"Harnessing social media is though few are clear on t ....gm , np, Mr. Lichtenwalner provides clarity and context on both fronts, and shows how the intelligent application of social media elevates brands and empowers leadership. If you're on the way up, read it carefully; if you're on the way down, read it quickly."
--- *Chris Cook, President: Fairly Painless Advertising*

"Explore how to meld social media with leadership practices and become a more effective leader. Everyone can benefit from the tools, techniques, and examples available in this book."
-- *Sandy Carter, IBM General Manager and Social Business Evangelist*

"Ben gets it. He understands what great service and leadership is all about and provides a guide for contemporary leaders to leverage technology for the benefit of their organizations. Paradigm Flip is a must read for modern servant leaders."
--Larry C. Spears, author-editor: *Insights on Leadership*, and *Fortuitous Encounters*

"I recruited Ben to join my NGO and speak at our fundraising events specifically because he exemplifies 'Servant Leadership' and the Paradigm Flip in today's hyper-digitally-connected world. Leaders today must master new channels of communication – and Ben's book will be your guide."
-- *Eric Melin, Founder: PHILANTHROPIST.org*

"How should leaders handle the challenges and opportunities of social media? Ben's strategies and tactics will inform you. But his underlying, implicit question and hypothesis will surprise and encourage you. They did me."
-- *Dr. Steve Vanderveen: Hope College, Center for Faithful Leadership*

"Ben truly understands social interactions across all channels. Paradigm Flip is a must read for any marketer wanting to connect with their audiences in the 'always on' era of the digital age. The social ecosystem of today is made up of personal interactions, non-personal communications and a deep-rooted belief that consumers own the brand – not the companies promoting them. Any leader looking to leverage word-of-mouth marketing and the power of the social sphere will flip out over Paradigm Flip."

> -- *Kurt Mueller, Chief Digital and Science Officer: Roska Healthcare*

"Ben clearly connects the power of servant leadership with the capabilities of social media. Every leader today should read this book."

> -- *Art Barter, Owner and Chairman: Datron World Communications and Founder and CEO: Servant Leadership Institute*

"There are many books that can teach you about leading people. There are many books that can teach you about the importance of social media and developing an effective platform for your message. However, there are no books presently that balance the enduring principles of servant-leadership with the ever-changing social media scene that have been designed to transform the individual, their immediate team, and their overall organization - until NOW! I highly recommend this work. Ben Lichtenwalner has done us a great favor in writing this book."

> -- *Tony Baron, Psy.D., D.Min, Azusa Pacific University Associate Professor of Christian Leadership & Formation Director, Graduate School of Theology in San Diego Author, "The Art of Servant Leadership" and "The Cross and the Towel"*

"If you are a leader, a servant leader, this is a book you will want to read. It blends some of the best of tried-and-true principles with a poignantly relevant approach to social media and technology. Get this book. Use it. Enjoy it."

> -- *Terry Brock, Marketing Coach, Author, Professional Speaker: TerryBrock.com*

PARADIGM FLIP

PARADIGM
FLIP

Leading People, Teams, and Organizations
Beyond the Social Media Revolution

Ben Lichtenwalner

A Radiant Forest, LLC Book
Holland, MI

Special thanks to the Hope College project team, including:

Senior Editors
Kara Robart
Katherine Sauer

Editors
Lydia Blickley
Hannah Gingrich
Chelsea Grainer
Hope Hancock
Kaitlyn Holmwood
Taylor Ann Krahn

Layout Design
Katherine Sauer

Dedications

For my Lord and Savior, Jesus Christ. Without His grace, I would not stand here today. For my wife and boys. Without their love and patience, this book would not be possible. For my parents. Without their love and values, I never would have learned these principles. And for fans of the Modern Servant Leader blog (ModernServantLeader.com). You inspire me to keep treading this trail. Keep serving.

CONTENTS

"One resists the invasion of armies; one does not resist the invasion of ideas." —Victor Hugo

FOREWORD

I develop leaders in business and in life. It's been my great fortune to work with executives in all types of organizations. In fact, I've had the opportunity to speak to audiences sized in the tens of thousands and to coach well-known leaders one-on-one. Therefore, I'm always on the lookout for innovative thinking on leadership development. So when I saw Ben's unique insights, I quickly became a fan.

Ben first began sharing his thoughts on leadership and technology about the time I published my second book *You Don't Need a Title to be a Leader*. But it wasn't until years later, after I spoke at the Chick-Fil-A Leadercast, that he and I met. Shortly after that conference, I noticed a spike in traffic to my website from ModernServantLeader.com—Ben's blog. I thanked him for his article on me, and we began a professional relationship that continues to this day.

Over the years I've often shared Ben's content with my clients as Ben shared mine with his readers. He interviewed me on my new books and the *Fred Factor* concept. I often felt our perspectives on authentic leadership principles were well-aligned. This was in part because he was well-versed on the great leadership innovators of our time and throughout history. Yet, there was something unique in what Ben advocated.

Ben's focus has never been solely on leadership principles, but also on the delivery of those principles. Often, in our circles, there are theorists who speak of what to believe more than how to deliver. Not so with Ben. He balances the "what" and the "how." I appreciate this about him and his work.

In the years since we met, social media has become increasingly popular. Nowadays, everyone is connected all the time, from executives checking status updates in line at the grocery store to teenagers texting before the movie. Ben is a digital native himself and has been in the trenches of social media from the beginning. As a result, it's no surprise he's the first to flesh out how leaders today can practice greater influence through social media. And he's done an excellent job of bringing insights to this phenomenon.

Paradigm Flip is a book for current and future leaders who want to know how advances in communication technology impact their role. In this book, Ben explains how you can connect the same great principles you always believed about leadership to the technology solutions of today. This is not a book that will be outdated next month, but one that explains the concepts our social media revolution delivered. These concepts will be around for decades to come and so too, I hope, will the principles advocated in this book.

I've followed Ben's writing for several years and enjoyed the many new ideas he advances in this book. If you want to improve your own leadership and better serve employees, volunteers, consumers and investors, you too will find great value in these pages. So I encourage you to read on and, as Ben would say, "keep serving…"

—Mark Sanborn, Author of *Fred Factor* and *You Don't Need a Title to be a Leader*

INTRODUCTION

This book is not about you. It will not make you filthy rich. It will not make your hair grow back or even turn a shade darker. After reading this, you won't suddenly be stronger or have the perfect family. No, this book is not about you.

Instead, this book is about your vision, mission, and organization. It is about how you can be a better leader to those you serve. The principles in this book address the timeless concepts of great leadership and place them in the context of contemporary mediums. The result is an opportunity to strengthen your leadership for the benefit of the people you serve.

No, this book is not about you. For books like that, please see the "Get Rich Quick" section of your nearest bookstore (do those still exist?). If, instead, you seek the achievement of your vision and that of your organization, then please read on.

Preview

Good, you're still with me. Before we dive into the book though, I want to give you a brief overview of what to expect. I've divided the contents into five major components. These sections are:

Social Media

Whether you're still new to the concept or you've been weaving your social media tapestry for years, we'll level set here. This is where I cover the basic concepts of social media, dispel common arguments against its benefits, and describe how the advances in digital communication change the way we work, play, and live. Finally, I close this section by explaining the timeless concepts of social media. These are the terms I will use throughout the book. For example, rather than mention specific sites by name, I'll talk about social media platforms. Instead of using one site's specific term of "likes," I'll talk about ratings and so on.

Leading People

This book is about people leadership, not industry or product leadership. Therefore, it's only fitting that I address how social media and leadership can align to help leaders serve people better. This section does just that. In "Leading People," I cover the major communication eras of leadership, from prehistoric man to digital social media. Then we look at some great examples, both positive and negative, of specific leaders using social media to connect with people. Finally, I wrap up this section by explaining what "veneer identities" are, why they are dying, and exploring the many aspects of trust required of contemporary leaders.

Your Platform

The platform is an important tool in every leader's toolbox. However, the evolution of the platform allows for a very different approach for modern leaders. This section covers the advances in publishing as they pertain to a leader's platform.

You'll also see why a strong platform is necessary and how to build one. Specifically, I dive into the three primary platform models: the Stronghold, Spider Web, and Hub and Spoke models. I wrap up by explaining the value of the platform, especially the benefits of connections, influence, listening tools, forums, and social proof.

Your Principles

This is the heart of the matter: the principles that successful leaders must follow in the social media revolution and beyond. I start by explaining this revolution. Then I walk you through each of the key principles: to Listen, to be Action-Oriented, to have Integrity, to Connect, to be Open, and to Serve. For each principle, I reflect on its practice during the American Revolutionary War and contemporary examples by leaders in the Social Media Revolution. My objective is to show that the value of these principles is timeless. What varies is how leaders practice these principles in each generation. Finally, because service is the cornerstone of all these principles, I expand on the concept of Servant Leadership and its importance for contemporary leaders.

Your Organization

This is all about your organization and leading your mission through the adoption of social media. To do this, I explain the stages of change your leadership must go through and provide sample policies and procedures. In addition, I look at how traditional jobs, like Marketing, Public Relations, Quality Assurance, and Human Resources have new responsibilities. Next, I look at the new roles being created by social media, including Community Managers and Brand Personas. I also discuss some tactical matters, like how to set up an effective communication station for your organization and how to create a social media playbook. Finally, I close out this last major section by explaining the power and potential of your team in the social media landscape.

Each major section includes a recap and reflection questions at the end. These may be used to help you reflect on your own leadership or as the basis of a group discussion.

You will also find quotes highlighted throughout the book. Each of these is associated with a Quick Response (QR) Code, like the one below. These QR Codes can be scanned with a phone's QR Code scanner to pull up more information relevant to that quote online. If you don't have a QR Code scanner on your phone, just search your App Store for "QR Code" or "QR Code Scanner" to find a free application you can use for this purpose.

Each QR Code will take you to a page on my website (ModernServantLeader.com) that was specifically created for that highlight. From the page, you will be able to:

1. Share the highlight with friends or colleagues online.
2. Find posts online that are related to that content.
3. Participate in a discussion on that topic.
4. Contact me for more information on the topic.

> *This book is not about you... it's about how you can be a better leader to those you serve.*

Now that you have an overview of what to expect, it's time to dive in. We begin our journey together with a short story based on a social media incident that I experienced not so long ago. Stories like this are everywhere. Some are worse than others. Most could be avoided with better leadership. For this and many more reasons, you should be interested in social media and how it enables, empowers, and, really, demands greater leadership.

Too Late on the Debate

As the senior eCommerce manager at the leading global appliance manufacturer, I have plenty on my plate. But one issue has perplexed me for a long time: our company's lack of investment in and planning around social media.

In fact, I've been building the case for social media for months and even running a rogue (dare I say, "renegade") team of social media advocates that we lovingly call the "Social Media Mavens." This rogue effort earns me the courtesy of a formal meeting with our Director of Digital Media, and I have my pitch ready.

Like us all, she seems well intentioned, but overburdened and understaffed. Still, I proceed with my pitch, which contains several recommendations, including:

1. Expanding the Reactive Monitoring Team

Me: "The reactive monitoring team has been doing a good job, but they could do a lot more. Right now, many of the comments they address have been identified and shared with them by other employees. There are still many posts going unaddressed. A more comprehensive tool, integrated with our Customer Relationship Management (CRM) software, will help avoid future misses and prevent costs or negative brand impact."

Director: "Yeah, I know."

2. Implementing a Proactive Monitoring Team

Me: "Today, we have no proactive monitoring team. When someone shares great news or positive reviews about one of our brands, we rarely encourage, share, or reinforce that message. Similar to the reactive monitoring space, we should have a team of proactive advocates to build brand awareness, loyalty, and positive sentiment online."

Director: "That would be great."

3. Guidelines for Third Parties

Me: "We have a lot of marketing agencies running our social media accounts. There need to be guidelines and standards for these third parties. For example, when something goes wrong, who do they contact? How do they raise awareness to our brand leaders about complaints or angry feedback received online?"

The Director's eyebrows raise at this point.

Me: "There have been many examples of major brand failures in social media. I'm sure you're familiar with how Chrysler's social media account said nobody in Detroit knew how to drive, or how Kenneth Cole offended Arabs with an insensitive post?"

I search her facial expression for any sign of familiarity, but the expression is flat, so I continue.

Me: "What if we experience a similar failure on our own social media accounts? What sort of expectations around fail-safes do we have? For example, do we require agency employees to separate personal and professional social media applications? Anyone with access to our official brand accounts should not access them from personal devices."

She seems interested, but lacks a sense of urgency.

Director: "Yep," she replies flatly, nodding in agreement, "but my hands are tied. We don't have the people or the budget. You do realize that our Senior Vice President (SVP) recently dismissed social media as a fad, right? How do you expect me to get funding?"

Me: "We must continue to push back. Nobody's presented the business case for social media to that SVP yet. We must present the facts, opportunities, and risks."

Director: "Perhaps. But I cannot commit to anything at this time."

Me: "Okay, give it some thought and let me know how I can support you in this endeavor. Let's connect again in a couple of weeks."

Director: "Sounds good."

My suggestions will be shockingly relevant within only a matter of hours. Still, neither of us can predict the chaos about to ensue.

Obama's Dead Grandmother

That night, I watch the presidential debate. In one of the closest presidential elections in history, there's bound to be a lot of people paying close attention—and a lot of discussion online.

In front of me on the coffee table is my laptop, open to my social media monitoring suite, where I have my usual streams of content running. These streams are columns of relevant social content across several social platforms, enabling me to see what people say about topics that interest me. The categories include:

- Friends and family
- Mentions of our brands or products
- Mentions of competitors and our industry
- Mentions of the term "Servant Leadership"

As I glance down at the streams, I notice the mentions of our brands spike suddenly. So I read the comments. My heart sinks as I see horrifying evidence that one of our official brand accounts has just sent an extremely offensive message:

> **Katy's Home Appliances**: Obama's grandma even knew it was going to be bad! She died 3 days before he became president. #nbcpolitics

I pause to pinch myself. Nope, this isn't a nightmare. Clearly an agency representative, thinking they were tweeting from their personal account, has sent a very inappropriate post from our Katy's Home Appliances[1] brand account. As a result, all our fans on that platform now think that our official company representative is suggesting that Obama's grandmother would prefer to die rather than live under his leadership—a statement likely to offend many Americans. That account currently has over thirty-one thousand followers. The NBC Politics hashtag ensures it is seen by thousands more who follow that topic. The replies, reposts, and shares of the original comment capture the eyes of many thousands more.

If the author had separate applications—one for personal and one for professional—this may not have happened. That is exactly what I had suggested earlier that very same day. Now social media is screaming with reactions, mostly of shock and dismay. Some people say they're throwing away our (perfectly good, several-hundred-dollar-value) products. Others swear off our brand for eternity and promise to inform their friends. Social media pundits already explain how this likely happened. Those same pundits show surprise that such a huge brand could not have controls in place to avoid the incident. The top blogs—both on politics and social media—post breaking news articles on the incident within minutes.

Several comments speak to the realization that this was likely just a mistake. Still many highlight that the ability for such a mistake to occur suggests that brand leadership does not adequately value or understand the power of social media.

"No!" I shout out loud as though someone were in the room listening. "We're trying, really we are. Don't blame the entire brand for one misinformed leader or a poorly managed employee."

There are countless posts piling up, and I feel helpless. I want to speak for the brand and apologize, but I'm not authorized to do so.

Eventually, I see an apology from the same brand account on the platform. Still, I wonder if our brand leadership is even aware of the incident. It is clear that the mistaken poster sent the apology and is trying to avoid further damage. It is not as clear whether they have notified senior leadership.

So I place a call to the same Digital Media manager that I spoke with just hours earlier. No answer. I text her. No response. I look for her on the company chat. No luck. So I go up one level to her boss, the Vice President accountable for the entire Katy's Home brand. She answers.

"Are you aware of what's happening?" I ask.

The words are barely out of my mouth when she responds, "Oh yeah, we're working on it. Thanks, Ben." I can hear the familiar sounds of a command center behind her. They've clearly got several people figuring out the best overall response. I hang up, only slightly relieved.

The whole incident reminds me of a poorly coached football team. Regardless of how great each individual player is, a single bad play can cost the entire game or even the season.

I think our coaches just don't understand how the game is played today. The coach could have recruited differently, adjusted the game plan to account for new rules, or designed better plays.

I trudge to bed that night with my mind racing. What will be our formal response? Who will send it? How will it happen? *How will leadership respond?*

The Outcome

Fighting for stronger social media support from our leadership was exhausting. This bad incident was just another case that could have been avoided. I was tired of fighting fires when we could be growing forests. I knew many organizations utilizing social media to drive benefits with consumers and employees alike. Companies like Zappos.com were empowering employees with social media accounts and encouraging them to engage customers directly. Those organizations were building brands, relationships, revenues, and leadership positions with social media while we reacted to our failures.

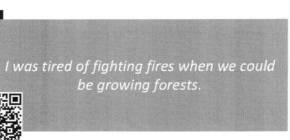

I was tired of fighting fires when we could be growing forests.

Never again did I want to be caught on the sidelines. I began gathering all my thoughts on how leaders should handle social media. These thoughts are captured here. I want you to see not only the risks, but also the incredible opportunity that is before you. You have something available to you that past leaders in history never had: advanced social media technology. What will you do with it?

There is a growing chasm between contemporary leaders, with those for and against social media on opposing sides. Those who are falling behind are stuck coping with failures or even non-existence. These organizations consider social media something to fear or claim that it is of no value. This is where my employer stood throughout the days of this incident. Leaders who excel in crossing this chasm use social media to build and strengthen their organizations. I want you to lead your organization to excellence with social media. This book is intended to help you leap over this chasm.

People who help their organization to cross this chasm and produce social media success will be the leaders of tomorrow. Their service, leadership, and guidance in the growing realm of digital collaboration will help pave the way for their mission's success.

Now you have a choice: You can turn a blind eye and think of social media as a fad, or you can read on and learn how this evolution in communication enables, empowers, and demands, from *you*, greater leadership.

SOCIAL MEDIA

"I must follow the people. Am I not their leader?"
—Benjamin Disraeli

Social media, in its purest form, is content surrounded by an interacting community. Advances in communication technology have catapulted the concept of social media to the forefront of society. After all, it is now easier than ever for communities to interact around content. As a result, there is rapidly growing awareness and opportunity in social media. In this section, I describe social media, the value it offers and how it impacts our lives. Before moving on, I'll also explain the universal concepts of social media that are used across all technologies and evolutions of the concept. I'll use those timeless terms through the remainder of the book.

How We Got Here

In early versions, social media was any meeting place where communities would gather to view and comment on activities. The Forum was a social media platform for the citizens in the early Roman Empire, where they gathered for everything from elections to gladiator matches. As technology evolved, so did our social media. With the printing press, communities began to gather and discuss the news at cafés.

The information revolution introduced digital platforms like Bulletin Board Systems, America Online, and Compuserve—the earliest versions of digital social media. Nowadays, there are thousands of digital social media platforms. These include the most popular social networks, professional platforms, online Wikis like the world's largest encyclopedia and thousands of community-maintained self-help guides. Although this concept is pervasive, still not everyone cares about social media.

The good news is that you're taking the time to read this, so you care at least a little. The bad news is that you will encounter detractors, like the executives who chose not to fund the ventures at my employer. This is a challenge you must overcome. If it's a battle you're struggling with, let's end it here. Here is why you (and your detractors) need to care about social media.

Sales professionals often have what is called a "rebuttal book." Such a book lists common excuses from prospective customers who don't want to buy a product. Under each excuse is a counter for that excuse. Consider this section your rebuttal guide. When you're standing in the elevator with your CEO and he asks whether that social media "stuff" you're working on is really just a fad, you had better be ready. Let's prepare for that elevator pitch.

Argument One: Social Media is a Fad

Opponents of social media perceive the technological advances and rapid adoption rates as nothing more than a "fad." Fad is defined by the Urban Dictionary as:[2]

> *A thing that becomes very popular in a short amount of time, and then is forgotten at about the same speed.*

Social media technologies have their origins in the virtual Bulletin Board Systems, or "BBS" for short, popularized in the 1990s. BBSs were online communities, driven mostly by discussion forums, before email and the World Wide Web hit mainstream media.

I grew up in the world of BBSs. It was an exciting time. I was able to make friends across the country, based on similar interests. So if social media traces back to BBSs and is expected to fade as fast as it arrived, you have at least a couple of decades before it goes away.

That said, social media is something we've been doing in person since the beginning of time. Communicating on a personal level, building trust, growing networks, sharing events—this is nothing new. What is new is the power afforded us through advances in technology. We can grow these interactions to a scale like never before. Here are two examples of social media from history, dating all the way back to prehistoric man.

Cave Drawings

One of the earliest documented forms of media was found in France. The Chauvet cave drawings are in Southern France and date back more than thirty thousand years.

Evidence from the cave suggests not only that there was community in the cave, but also that the paintings evolved— being edited, updated, or modified several times over thousands of years. This suggests that humankind, shortly after discovering the benefits of an opposable thumb, began sharing media in a social community.

> *Social media is something we've been doing in person since the beginning of time.*

Ancient Egyptian Hieroglyphics
Ancient Egyptians customized versions of books for people at their death. The Book of the Dead, or the "Book of Going Forth by Day," contained texts such as spells, homages, and speeches that deceased relatives might find useful in the afterlife. The Papyrus of Ani is one such example. In this example, we see that ancient Egyptians already appreciated the value of building on previous content, adapting it for personal use, and sharing it for the benefit of the community.

What Has Changed
Social media, in and of itself, is not a new concept. What is new is the evolution of the technology, which enables your community to expand on a global scale. As a result, the power of greatest communication has shifted from a centralized point of control to the masses. This is why leaders should be so passionate about social media: great leadership is no longer just an ideology, but a demand from the masses.

The expectation for great leadership has also always existed. After all, who would desire bad leadership? However, advances in social media technology have given the masses a voice. Leadership is no longer something that can be concealed behind closed doors. The expectations of the masses can no longer be ignored. The voice of the community is there for the world to see. The moment a leader is caught failing in his or her responsibilities, the community engages in a massive dialogue and demands a response to that failure.

The result ranges from a call for an apology, such as in the case of poor taste by brand executives, to massive revolts, such as we see now in the Arab Spring. In minor incidents, leaders must apologize and correct themselves, or the masses take their interest, purchasing power, and support elsewhere. In major incidents, such as political tyranny in the Middle East, masses of people can no longer be silenced, and autocratic leaders are chased out of the country.

Great leadership is no longer just an ideology, but a demand from the masses.

Social media did not drive this shift in power. The technology evolution of social media principles simply enabled what was always desired.

Bottom Line

Social media is nothing new. The concept dates back to prehistoric man. Major technology advances in social media have been around for a couple decades now. In essence, they empower what we already did in person but on a larger scale. However, by leveraging the latest tools, we can maximize our capacity and scale like never before.

Argument Two: Social Media Lacks a Return on Investment

Another popular argument is the perceived lack of a Return on Investment (ROI). ROI is essentially a fancy business term for how much you profit from an investment. If you claim no ROI, an investment of ten dollars will not produce more than ten dollars in return. The problem with this lack of ROI argument is threefold:

1. Traditional Media Lacks ROI

The argument of inadequate ROI often comes from marketing executives opposed to change. The hypocrisy in this statement is the historical lack of measurable ROI in traditional marketing. How does the marketing executive know that a billboard leads to sales? She doesn't. When was the last time you actually sat and watched the commercials on your favorite television show? In fact, there's been a fifty percent decline in television viewership in recent years.[3] Yet somehow we're suddenly so concerned about the ROI of social media? I personally like the way Gary Vaynerchuck summarized this concern:[4]

> " . . . What's the ROI of Social Media? . . . What's the ROI of your mother?! . . . The ROI of my mother is everything . . . However, I can't show you, in data, the ROI of my mother . . . Social's gonna prove it. Because social has way better metrics than traditional."
> —Gary Vaynerchuk

But ROI is just one measurement. Social media is more measurable than traditional media in many ways.

2. Social Media is More Measurable

What traditional media lacked in measurability, social media has in excess. If you want to know how many people your message reached, it's easy to track that data via web traffic reports. If you want to tie sales to a marketing campaign, you can count exactly how many users click each link. Leaders seeking to measure the sentiment of their followers can even use reporting tools to provide reasonably accurate metrics. Everything in digital social media can be measured to an extent. The challenge is that achieving that measurement requires some investment.

> *Everything in digital social media can be measured to an extent.*

Investing in Measurement

Because technology evolves rapidly, the tools for measuring social media ROI evolve faster than tools in traditional fields. Therefore, anyone who complains about a lack of ROI must understand the need to invest in the ability to measure its impact.

Anyone suggesting there is no ROI in social media misunderstands the problem. The real challenge is not a lack of ROI, but the necessity of investing up front to ensure comprehensive and accurate tracking of that ROI. The same challenge exists with any investment. However, older technologies and traditional media have a plethora of long-accepted tools for this purpose. This is a convenience not shared with social media. Regardless, with the right planning and budgeting, social media ROI can be tracked and reported better than most other investments.

3. There's More to Success than ROI

I have a big, fancy (and expensive) Master's Degree in Business Administration (MBA), which obligates me to respect ROI. My even fancier degree from the school of hard knocks, also known as "common sense," obligates me to recognize that successful organizations do not depend upon ROI alone. If we only invested in products and services that presented an immediate ROI business case, here are some investments that never would have been made:

- **Light Bulb**: With the lack of proliferated electricity, most investors suggested that nobody would want to buy a product they couldn't (yet) use.
- **Wikipedia**: Wikipedia depended upon volunteer time, yet it blew away the well-funded Encarta.
- **Automobile**: The early days of the automobile suggested a much more costly venture than a couple of horses.
- **Personal Computer**: In the early days of computers, many people saw no value for the technology in homes.

Bottom Line

Measuring the ROI of social media requires some investment. That said, it is much easier to measure the impact of social media than it is to measure traditional media, like television, radio, and print advertising. The key is planning to invest in that measurement because the technology in this space is comparatively new.

Argument Three: We Don't Have Time for Social Media

For the individual opposed to social media, another common complaint is a lack of time to use emerging social media technologies. Yet through a single post on one network, you can reach all interested people.

Sure, email can do that, but you can't effectively email the world and let the world filter what's important. Social media tools enable this type of behavior. Through opt-ins, keyword searches, communities, and ratings, it's easier than ever for people to find the most relevant content and filter out the rest.

The same is true, of course, for your fans and subscribers. The most popular and relevant content is quickly raised or lowered, depending upon preferences and the weightings of reviews. In essence, social media consumers use—and expect their connections to use—filters. Not every post is expected to be read by everyone. Each user's filters set the tone on what is consumed. As a result, social media technologies are arguably the most efficient communication tools available today.

Email use decreases as each new generation enters the workforce. The shortest format message is preferred. Therefore, a lack of social media engagement decreases your relevance to the next generation.

Social media technologies are time savers, not wasters. Filters, professional networks, and communities all result in greater efficiencies. For example, a filter enables you to see only the content you're interested in from a broad community. Professional networks empower you to find resources and solutions that worked for others thus reducing trial-and-error. Similarly, communities allow leaders to group communications by interest area. If you're still unconvinced, try it for a month, and I promise you'll see the time-saving benefits.

Bottom Line

When done right, social media saves people time. If we're not engaged in social media when our employees, volunteers, and customers are, it will cost extra time to get the message to them through other channels.

A lack of social media engagement decreases your relevance to the next generation.

If you still think social media is a fad, lacks ROI, or consumes too much time, consider the following numbers (note that these numbers are at time of first publication and will likely have increased by the time the book hits shelves):

Social Media, the Time-wasting Fad with no ROI

Caution: You are entering the sarcasm zone. Sometimes we need to be confronted with the brutal facts, rather than subjective opinions. As Jim Collins said in *Good to Great*,[5] one key characteristic of a great leader is their ability to "confront the most brutal facts of your current reality." So if the following section seems sarcastic, keep in mind that we want to confront the brutal facts and put subjective detractors to rest.

The leading social platform,[6] at the time of this writing, has over one billion users.

> FAD: One billion sounds like a small number—I'm sure it will fade away.
> ROI: There could not possibly be any value in reaching one billion people, could there?
> TIME: I'm sure the one billion people using the leading platform are not nearly as busy as you are.

The world's largest encyclopedia,[7] entirely online, was created through the social collaboration of millions of users, all working for free. If printed, this encyclopedia would produce over two million pages.

> FAD: Clearly, social media is not producing anything of value, so it will disappear soon.
> ROI: The fact that people create over two million pages of content for free does not suggest any real value or cost savings.
> TIME: It seems time spent online is all wasted on irrelevant information.

Nielsen, the great market survey company, reports that trust in paid advertising is down to forty-two percent, and ninety-two percent of consumers prefer insights from friends and family.[8]

> FAD: The fact that consumers prefer reviews from friends and family to those from marketers must be a fad.
> ROI: Ninety-two percent of consumers prefer recommendations from those they know; investing in that must not be valuable.
> TIME: I'm sure you're too busy to address your consumer's needs.

Sarcasm aside, I hope it's clear by now that social media is not a time-wasting fad that lacks ROI. As time passes, we will see billions of people on these platforms. These communities are producing great value on topics that interest them for little or no cost. The evolution of social media technologies enables users to get facts from actual consumers, moving trust away from organizations and into the community itself. It seems the only time-wasting fad with a lack of ROI is the fad not to invest in social media.

Traditional Media's Role

Is traditional media an endangered species on the brink of extinction? Hardly. However, its value is drastically diminished. Gary Vaynerchuk also pointed out in one of his presentations that billboards have lost their significance because fewer and fewer people read them. He described how it's scary to see so many people texting while driving and the implications that has on billboards: "People aren't looking at billboards, they aren't even looking at the freakin' road anymore." Vaynerchuk further explained that traditional media is being proven less cost effective.

In his book *Crush It!,* [9] Vaynerchuk explained a simple experiment that he ran. In this experiment, he invested $7,500 in a billboard and $15,000 in direct mail. He then shared the same offer in social media. The billboard brought in three hundred orders, and direct mail brought two hundred.

Social media brought him seventeen hundred orders . . . in less than forty-eight hours. Cost? $0.

If you want to create support for your mission, paid advertising is expensive, less trusted, and ultimately less effective. Direct connections and even indirect messages through common networks are far more motivating. This is an example of the powerful influence available through social media.

But not everybody is online, and not everybody has such a loyal follower base. In a presentation on the *Zero Moment of Truth (ZMOT)*, [10] Jim Lecinski from Google explained that traditional media is still critical for the impulse it generates. Print publications, television, and radio: these all serve a great purpose for the impulse. They inspire stakeholders to take an action. They pique the curiosity and motivate people to find your product, service, or leadership online. And that is the fundamental difference.

Traditional media marketing used to be the decision-factor. You'd create the purchasing desire with traditional media, motivating the consumer to go to the store and buy the product. This is no longer the case. Traditional media now serves the singular purpose of inspiring the inquiry.

People don't make decisions based on traditional advertising channels anymore. "Stanley Homemaker" doesn't see an ad in his *Gentleman's Home Journal* and say, "Oh, well, if they advertise in *Gentleman's Home Journal*, it must be the product for me, so I'm going to the store to buy me a Gladiator® Premier Tool Chest." No, instead he sees the ad and his interest is piqued. He then pulls his tablet off the workbench and searches online for "Gladiator Premier Tool Chest." If he's particularly savvy, he may even search for "Gladiator Premier Tool Chest Reviews" or "Gladiator Premier Tool Chest Comparison." If he's intrigued by what he finds, he asks his network of contacts online, "Anybody using this, and if so, what do ya think?"

The same is true for your prospective team members. Recruits interested in your organization are not going to take your word for it if they do not know you. They trust their connections. Similarly, prospective team members trust strangers and their bias-free opinions over anything published by your organization.

When traditional media was once the decision point, it had greater value and therefore cost more. Now, the same dollars that went to the point of inspiration and decision in traditional media must be split. Instead, only some of those dollars should go to traditional media to pay for the inspiration, and some of those dollars should go to new media for the point of decision. Google terms this point of decision The Zero Moment of Truth.

> *Traditional media now serves the singular purpose of inspiring the inquiry.*

As a leader, you need to understand this shift in where people are influenced. It may help your organization's marketing, but it will also help your influence. These same principles apply to your messaging. Buying lots of traditional media, print advertising, or banner ads online will only inspire the inquiry.

Instead, work on influencing the influencers. Find the people in your organization and beyond that have great influence with others. Then get those influencers on board. That said, social media changes more than just the way we are influenced. This is the world we live in. Advances in social media technology are changing the way we work, play, and live.

The Way We Work

We don't work the way we did just five years ago. Sure, the realization of the Internet changed a lot. Evolution in our communication technology changes a whole lot more. Social media changes how we collaborate internally and externally, how we find work, and how we find and hire others.

1. Internal Collaboration

Employees, contractors, and volunteers find it easier than ever to connect and collaborate more effectively. There are countless examples, but one landmark case was corporate Goliath, IBM's "Beehive." Beehive was IBM's internal collaboration suite à la social network. Through Beehive, employees shared common interests, top challenges of their projects, key areas of research, and subject matter expertise. This enabled IBM's four hundred thousand or more employees to quickly find each other and others who could help. Said IBM's Liam Cleaver:[11]

> "You cannot create a culture of innovation without creating a culture of collaboration—and at its core it (Beehive) is creating a culture of trust with people you may never have met."

As a leader in your organization, look to companies like IBM for examples of internal collaboration. Sure, you may not have the resources of this global giant, but technology is increasingly cheaper. Today, there are very inexpensive options for you to consider, both for internal collaboration as well as external.

Employees, contractors, and volunteers find it easier than ever to connect and collaborate more effectively.

2. External Collaboration

Public platforms offer similar opportunities for external collaboration. In the old world, someone seeking a subject matter expert had to contact several, if not dozens of people before they found an expert. Now a quick search online will tell you not only who that expert is, but also:

- How you are connected
- How many years of experience the expert has
- Where he or she is located
- Whether he or she is open to new connections
- How consumers of the expert's service rate his or her knowledge, skills, and performance
- And much more . . .

Many of these public platforms are free or "freemium" solutions. A freemium solution is free to use the basic features, with licensing fees for more advanced capabilities. For example, if your information can be shared publicly, the free options may suffice. If you need the option of collaborating behind closed doors, you may have to pay a fee for such a solution.

3. Job Search

Hitting the pavement is obviously a thing of the past. Now the best employees are querying their friends and professional network. They ask:

"Do you know anyone who is hiring?"
"How do you enjoy working for your employer?"

Of course, candidates may not have direct, personal connections to the target employer. No matter, there are plenty of complete strangers willing to give detailed, firsthand accounts of the organization. So candidates hop over to any number of sites where current employees provide open, anonymous feedback on the organization. Details provided include: average salaries, benefit options, culture perspectives, and more. In fact, many sites even include recommendations that the anonymous employees have for the executive leadership and very specific ratings. If you want to find what your employees suggest to you, try a simple web search for your company name and "executive ratings" or "employee reviews."

Candidates who want to know how a prospective employer stacks up against their competition or even the candidate's current employer can conduct a very specific comparison. In fact, when candidates are considering potential employers, that company's website is often the last stop. Instead, the first stop for candidates is frequently their professional networks or employer review websites. The company website is often not viewed until they need facts for the interview.

4. Hiring

Now, the traditional résumé carries less weight as well. Hiring managers and their Human Resources departments usually don't even start with the résumé. Instead, they begin with their professional network online:

"Who do I know that may know someone for this role?"
"Who else may I know that I'm not thinking of?"

This is one reason many employers look to future leaders for the strength of their network. The more professional connections a person has, the better. This used to be identified by their experience. Did the individual have an executive MBA from a top ten business school? Great! They must know a lot of people they can pull in, as needed.

Now an MBA is less impressive than a strong, quantifiable network of quality connections. A piece of paper representing years of study weighs less than knowing an executive who has direct connections with board members at several of your top customers. The MBA is subjective and assumption-based. The social network is fact-based and measurable. This data is, of course, now readily available.

As a leader in this generation, you can use this information to your benefit. Make sure your digital network represents you well. When looking to connect with a new organization, reach out to connections in that company and their customers. Try looking at board members or other senior leaders and their public networks. If you can't connect with them directly, perhaps you can reach a shared connection.

> *Now an MBA is less impressive than a strong, quantifiable network of quality connections.*

Digital Shadows

Then there is the dreaded social history. Every candidate has a digital shadow that could reflect a positive or negative history. Fraternity brothers who were so proud of their keg-stand record and the many photos of their crowning achievements now regret that so many people shared those moments online. Or that Spring Break when it was so funny that you entered and won the hairiest back contest—that may not be so impressive to executive recruiters.

"Don't do anything you don't want printed on the front page," is now, "Don't do anything you don't want shared on a social media platform." As a leader, one regrettable moment will quickly become the first search result for anyone researching you or your organization. The best way to avoid this is not to wait to address that bad moment when it happens, but to prepare in advance. High levels of positive online engagement will help ensure positive search results long before a bad incident. At worst, you'll see plenty of positive to balance the negative.

Specialized Searches

Getting people to do work for you is also easier than ever before. This is true whether you seek a software programmer or a babysitter. When you needed a babysitter in the past, your personal network was your only hope for a romantic night out with the hubby. Now, there are specialized sites that list, rate, and review countless childcare professionals in your neighborhood.

The resources do not end with babysitters, of course. The same holds true for senior care, appliance repair, manual labor, and offshore personal assistants. For each specialized skill set, there is a resource available to help you find qualified candidates.

The connections and digital shadow of candidates, combined with specialized search tools, change the way we hire. These changes, along with how we collaborate and search for jobs ourselves, are all changing the way we work. But social media's not just changing how we work; it's also changing how we play.

The Way We Play

When personal computers and email first entered the scene, technology was perceived to reduce personal interaction. Now, we realize that, thanks to technology, we are more personal than ever before. Those comfortable with the technology are able to communicate on a personal level with more people than ever possible in the past. Specifically, we're now able to find each other, share media, coordinate meetings, and even play games together through social media.

1. Finding Each Other

Old college and high school friends are reconnecting with ease. Prior to the evolution of social networks, tracking down an old acquaintance took days, weeks, or even years. The searcher had to start with a phone call or letter to the closest shared contact. If that didn't work, there might have been another person recommended to contact. So another phone call or letter was needed and on and on, until hopefully, one day, the connection was re-established.

Today, of course, this search is much more simple. A quick search term, and bang, the searcher has all people matching that name in their network and beyond, listed at their fingertips. Common name? No problem. The searchers can quickly drill down based on where people live, how they are connected, and what organizations they are associated with.

As leaders, this is an important tool for building your support base, whether you want to surround you and your team with friends, or simply use the friends and family network for seed funding or donations. We trust those we know best, and often those are old friends. Use your network to reach out to a support base.

2. Sharing Media
When I was a toddler, it was a big deal to record new words my siblings and I learned on audiocassette and mail them to my grandparents. On occasion, we'd even make the expensive, long-distance call to speak with them directly. But that was the extent of our media. My extended family, who lived a one- or two-day drive away, had to imagine what we looked like while hearing our voices and wait for photos in the mail that arrived weeks after the original photo was taken.

Now, letters, photos, and videos can be shared immediately. Better yet, I enjoy video chats with the great-grandparents of my children. Over the course of one generation, we've gone from weeks between a photo being taken, developed, and shipped to real-time, two-way streaming video for free.

As a leader, you may be placing fathers and mothers on the road for weeks at a time. Ensure they are equipped with the technology to make these connections simple and frequent. Your people will appreciate your concern for them and their families.

3. Coordinating Meetings
Are you planning a destination wedding with hundreds of guests or arranging a convention of professional tax advisors in southwest Michigan? "There's an app for that." TM Seriously, it's easier than ever to convene groups of similar interests of all shapes and sizes. From the casual, impromptu "meet up" to the large corporate conference.

Selecting the date, location, food, content, even the attire of guests can be easily facilitated through collaboration and democracy. Everyone has a say in the program and therefore a sense of ownership for participation. Benchwarmers are still welcome to pay and attend, but the bulk of attendees are now active contributors.

As a leader, you will undoubtedly have to coordinate many meetings. Consider how those you work with can participate in this process. Use the many tools available to make them active participants in determining when a meeting is needed, as well as how, when, and where to have that meeting.

Also, think beyond the traditional scope of team meetings. Why only meet with employees? Why not send an open invite to meet consumers, volunteers, or fans? You will build a great deal of goodwill by being accessible in person.

4. Playing Games

Whether you're the kind of person who loves the first-person shooters full of explosions, prefers a civil game of chess, or is somewhere in between, your games have evolved. You are no longer alone. The first-person shooter used to be for pimple-faced, social rejects . . . well, I guess the same could have been true for chess players, but I digress . . .

Now, everyone's online, connected, and interacting. The human element is back. It's not about being alone in a dark room with a computer. Instead, it's about interaction among game players. Coordination in what used to be simple "blast them all away" games is suddenly important. Coordination of team members is now a pervasive element of games. Individual gamers are gaining teamwork experience online, where they often join forces, practice together, and compete in tournaments. The result is a greater emphasis on teamwork in every setting.

This concept of collaboration extends beyond what we traditionally consider games to many platforms. Points and rewards for checking in at a location rank you on leader boards. The more reviews you offer, the more perks you get.

Gamification is in facets of everything we do in the workplace, thus enabling the human competitive spirit to drive greater results.

In fact, there are many books that focus on the benefits video games now provide players. Author and game designer Jane McGonigal believes game playing could save the world.[12] According to McGonigal, we currently spend about three billion hours per week playing online games, but that's not enough.

> *"If we want to solve problems like hunger, poverty, climate change, global conflict, obesity . . . I believe that we need to aspire to play games online for at least twenty-one billion hours per week by the end of the next decade."—Jane McGonigal at TED2010*

McGonigal goes on to explain how we are often the best version of ourselves in the game world. The intense concentration we have, the persistence in tackling challenges after repeated failure, an overall sense of "I can do this": these attributes often seem absent in "the real world." As we see "the real world" and online gaming merge closer and closer together, we're growing closer to harnessing the tremendous power of video games to solve real world problems. In fact, we have an idea how many hours of game play we need, per person, thanks to Malcom Gladwell.

Malcom Gladwell's ten thousand hour theory of success in his book *Outliers* suggests that to be masterful at a skill, you must practice it for ten thousand hours.[13] McGonigal points out that this is the same number of hours students spend in school between fifth grade and high school graduation in the United States. It is also, McGonigal says, the number of hours that the average youth spends playing video games by the time they are twenty-one.

Social interaction over video games teaches our teams to solve problems together. So, if video game players are becoming experts at solving problems in a virtual world and they are more socially connected than ever before, they're becoming world leaders at solving problems through teamwork. This suggests that leaders should take a fresh look at video games, the people who play them, and the skills developed as a result. Where video game play, in general, was once a negative, it should now be considered a positive under the right circumstances.

Don't look at employees who play games as time wasters, but as team builders who appreciate clear incentives. Consider how points, rewards, trial-and-error, and other gamer attributes can help grow your business and the interests of your team.

First we saw how social media changes the way we work. Here we saw how it changes the way we play and its implications for leaders. Through advances in social media technology, people are finding each other more easily, coordinating meetings with ease, sharing more media faster, and building teamwork skills through gameplay. But it doesn't stop with how we work and how we play. How we work and play combine to comprise how we live.

The Way We Live

Social media is blurring the lines between how we work and play. For the leader ready to embrace this change, this is a welcome balance. To see this all play out in one space, imagine the following scenario, with yourself as the business leader at the center of the story.

Surroundings

You sit in a room surrounded by giant digital screens. These screens vary in size, color, and placement. Some are labeled and include the names of your best friends, family members, and coworkers. Some even have the names of competitors. The screens that are labeled reflect content from those people and organizations only.

The screens which are not labeled include names on each new piece of content that appears. These are the generic screens and seem to mostly contain information from strangers. For example, as a piece of content appears on one it immediately lists the source, such as this:

> "Just had a great meal from the new chain that just moved into town. Wow, so glad they're here now!"— John D. Foodie

You guess there are several hundred screens in all, spread across this large room in which you now sit. Yet they don't seem obtrusive.

The chair you use is also remarkably comfortable. You have a personal waiter attending to your every need. If you want, you can switch on any movie, television show, or music inside any screen.

You have your favorite music playing and a veritable "personal top ten" video stream on. If you prefer to exercise, there is a virtual trainer there, complete with treadmill, exercise bike, and elliptical machine. The room temperature hovers at your perfect setting, and the ambient lighting is just the way you want it. If there's anything you want, your waiter gets it.

As you recline in your chair or hop on that treadmill, you begin to watch your screens, occasionally glancing at the video streams. Your attention goes first to the family and friends screens.

First, your spouse's stream grabs your attention—she's frustrated at work. It seems that same antagonist has reared her ugly head again. Next, you see some new photos appear—your cousin just got married, and wow, what a looker his new spouse is!

The Review

Out of the corner of your eye, you catch the word "toaster" and remember that you need to get a new one because yours recently died. The post is from your friend Nathan.

Nathan just bought a new toaster and loves it. It has several advanced features but, more importantly, it is constructed of quality material. Since your last toaster died after only six months, you're intrigued and follow the link he shared.

While browsing the site you see that the toaster has excellent reviews. Over one hundred thirty people rated it—most with four out of five stars or better. You notice the closest competing product has an average of only two and a half stars. It seems that this is clearly the toaster you want. As a busy executive, you value your time, so you place the order online and have it shipped to your office.

Over the span of five minutes, you reviewed feedback from your trusted friend and over one hundred thirty other people, selected the product, purchased it, and feel confident with the results. No need to even consider other options. With that to-do item checked off, you return to watching your video stream.

At the bottom of the screen, you see an alert from an unknown user. Your automated search filter picked up on one of your predefined keywords. Somebody is furious about one of your company's products.

This complaint specifically calls out your product by name and brand. Following several expletives on bad quality, the complaint states that the Customer Service was also horrible.

Concerned, you follow a link to the user's profile. As you read the full review, you notice his major complaints were with a particular part that failed two days after the warranty expired.

The unhappy customer goes on to say that he then had to wait on hold with your (newly outsourced) Customer Service department for over fifteen minutes. As you read the review, you notice the customer's post being praised by many users. Several comments were already added that include:

- "I had that same part go bad on mine!" #ACMEFail—@JDoe
- "Me too! What a piece of junk!" #ACMEFail—@EBryce
- "Same here—should we start a class action?!" #ACMEFail—@BizRvw1
- "Has anybody found a solution other than calling the service department?! I can't wait 15 minutes on hold . . . " #ACMEFail—@BByDdy11
- "Wow, I'm never buying that brand again" #ACMEFail—@JustInTimePR
- "Such a shame—they used to be a great company" #AcmeFail—@NvrNvrLand

You stop reading and recognize the hashtag (#ACMEFail) as a common keyword identifier used online. By including your company name, "Acme," and "Fail," anyone who ever wants to find comments about any of your failures will see this among the results.

Is anyone in Public Relations or Marketing reading this, you wonder? We need to stop this downward spiral of negativity. Is anyone defending your product? You know the Research and Development team planned to replace that part in future models because it was poorly made and not up to the specifications your engineers sent the manufacturer. Who will relay this to the customers?

You also know there was a twenty-five cent replacement part that could be ordered—the outsourced call center was supposed to know that and offer it as an option . . . why weren't they? Come to think of it, the call center had a Service Level Agreement (SLA) for five minutes hold time or less. Who was tracking their progress against that SLA? If they have failed to meet the agreement, you know there are discounts due.

Frustrated, you send an email:

To: Erica (VP of Public Relations); Jacob (Director of Engineering); Johnathan (Director of Customer Service)
Subject: Social Outbreak For Our New Widget
Message:

All,

I found this review of our product and the disappointed customers <you include a link here>. It seems to be gaining popularity. Three questions:

1. Who is monitoring this, and where are they?
2. When do improved products hit the shelves?
3. Is the new call center meeting their SLAs?

Thanks,
—You

Marketing Campaign

You notice that it's getting late, and the game you wanted to watch is about to start. Before turning off most of the screens, you decide to check in on your new "Going Green Campaign." You committed a boost to the budget for the program sixty days ago, and you want to see if the public's opinion has improved.

You pull up a screen designated with the "green" label and search for your brand's name. Hmmm . . . No results. You try again under the screen labeled "Macatawa," the name of the town where you're building a new, totally Green facility. Sure enough, there's a long list of results. Comments include:

- "New complex by Acme sounds really impressive—first in the area to meet the LEED^{TM} standard. I'm cautiously optimistic!" #Macatawa—@Gr33nLant3rn

- "Yeah, they're making an effort—still not sure if they're sincere about it or not though. They have a lot of facilities with plenty of waste. One site is only a small step." #Acme #Macatawa #Environment—@Nevea24

Then you're thrilled to see a member of your team in the conversation:

- "@Nevea24—You're right, we still have much work to do! However, our legacy buildings are also investing in waste reduction—read more here <she includes a link>" #Macatawa—@AcmeJane (Employee)

- "Cool—thanks Jane. Just read it and I am impressed. Glad to see your company investing here—I'll be sure to promote your products to my friends!" #Macatawa—@Nevea24

Jane has always been a passionate promoter of your green initiatives and is actively spreading the message. You know the link she referenced, confident that the customer would be happy to see the additional efforts made in waste control. Comfortable and confident, you turn off most of the screens, leaving on only the streaming game, your friends and family, and internal work stream. During commercials, you check up on the latest from each . . .

Real Value Examples

Perhaps you're not in business, but a pastor instead. Therefore, you're not checking up on the construction of a plant, but on the community dialogue about job closings. Or maybe you're a community activist opposed to a new ordinance that would eliminate green space. Whatever your passion, it can be followed, shared, and influenced on social media channels.

This is very much like social media today. No, it is not a magic room with dedicated waiters or giant screens. However, it is anywhere and everywhere you want it to be.

While you may not have a waiter, you can have social media in your hands while waiting at your favorite restaurant. While the room you're in right now may not be the perfect temperature, you can take social media with you to the beach or the ski lift. Social media is ubiquitous.

Social media replaces much of what traditional media once provided. Now, people listen to traditional marketing channels less. They would rather hear from friends, family, and unbiased strangers. Therefore, it matters less what you as the leader say, but you can influence the conversation. You are valued more now for providing facts, clarifying issues, or otherwise offering support. In the world of social media, your stakeholder is your primary, and often only, marketer.

Whatever your passion, it can be followed, shared, and influenced on social media channels.

Power Shift

Historically, power was concentrated in a few individuals at the top of any organization. As a result, information was power, and autocratic or top-down leadership models dominated the workplace. Now, evolutions in social media technology have upended this power consolidation.

Information is still powerful. However, instead of that information being easily controlled and contained, it's amassed for the masses. Everyone with an interest can see the one negative review a single consumer shares online. This complaint could be from one out of a million consumers, but every prospective buyer researching your product can see it.

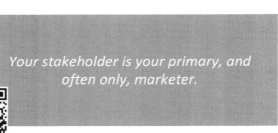

Your stakeholder is your primary, and often only, marketer.

Is it fair for the producers? Nope. Was it fair that the producers had all the power over consumers for centuries? Definitely not. The masses are revolting. This power shift represents the social media revolution. Employees are no longer to be managed, but led. Consumers are no longer to be pushed toward a product or service, but pulled in. Stakeholders are no longer an afterthought, but the first thought. Leaders can no longer serve themselves, but must serve others. This is the social media revolution: the shifting of power from the few at the top to the many they serve. The power is now in the hands of all your stakeholders.

Know Your Stakeholders

I've now mentioned stakeholders several times. I want to clarify my meaning of the word because you'll hear about them a lot.

Today, leaders have many different constituents. You may be in business and serving your investors, consumers, and employees. These are all stakeholders. You may be in politics and therefore serving your constituents, political party members, and those impacted by your legislature. These are all examples of a politician's stakeholders. Or you may be a teacher, serving students and parents as your stakeholders. The non-profit executive serves employees, philanthropists, and beneficiaries of their services as stakeholders. In short, a stakeholder is anyone you serve with your leadership. In social media, your connections are also stakeholders.

It is important to maintain this broad focus on stakeholders because successful leadership requires a leader to serve many stakeholder groups. Today, many failures of leadership can be traced back to a singular focus on one stakeholder group. For an example, see the "Bob Nardelli" section under "Serve" in the chapter on "Your Principles."

This is the social media revolution: the shifting of power from the few at the top to the many they serve.

Advances in social media technology highlight the degree to which a leader does or does not serve different stakeholder groups. For instance, a leader who does an excellent job serving investors will cause the stock price to rise—for a short period of time. However, if cuts in quality damage product performance, evidence of disgruntled consumers will quickly accumulate online through bad product reviews. Because this leader chose to serve investors at the cost of consumers, he has failed to serve the organization as a whole. This is where the power shift has a great impact. Stakeholders now control the power.

> *"There is only one boss. The customer. And he can fire everybody in the company from the chairman on down, simply by spending his money somewhere else."*
> —Sam Walton

Where necessary, the stakeholders will stage a revolt. In fact, this is why we are in the social media revolution. While you may not fight with bullets and spill blood, you should be aware of the weapons and what is at stake.

Instead of information being easily controlled and contained, it's amassed for the masses.

Whatever your role in an organization happens to be, chances are that the company has less power over stakeholders than it did ten years ago. This power shift is due to the evolution of social media technology. Leading in this world with a new balance of power requires an understanding of timeless concepts. Although these key concepts have been around for centuries, many leaders have ignored them. These concepts can no longer be ignored.

Timeless Social Media Concepts

Before we dig into the core concepts of leading over social media, I want to take a moment to reflect on this timeless concept of social media. That's right, I said "timeless" and "social media" in the same sentence. Here's why:

This is the curse that any author seeking to touch on—let alone write a book on—social media must face. It's the curse of obsolescence. By the time I finish writing this book, I guarantee at least one currently popular social media product will be obsolete. That's why I tend not to talk about the technology itself.

As technologies evolve, products will appear and disappear. However, the concepts are timeless, even if the technologies are dated. Here are the enduring concepts of social media:

Platforms

In the days of cavemen, as we discussed earlier, the platform was the cave wall. It was the canvas on which the message was created, viewed, shared, and updated. Paper became another platform. Email lists, listserves, America Online, Compuserve, Prodigy, and bulletin board systems (BBSs) were early forms of digital platforms. Since the popularization of the term "social media," more popular platforms include blogs (web logs), MySpace, Facebook, LinkedIn, Pinterest, Twitter, QZone, Orkut, and more. The platform often sets the terminology that is used for the rest of the concepts below.

In the future, digital platforms will be more ubiquitous, likely integrated with, if not the foundation of, operating systems embedded in your home appliances, automobiles, and more. Through wearable technology embedded in eyeglasses, watches and other accessories, augmented reality will seamlessly integrate your virtual social media with the physical world. These platforms will be entirely customized to your preferences, especially the user interfaces. As a result, you'll have your social media platform with you everywhere you go, in the most familiar format, with completely tailored content.

Connections

It's great to be popular, isn't it? Connections help us feel that way. Whether your platform calls them friends, followers, subscribers, fans, reviewers, pals, or any other term, they are your connections. These are individuals who request and receive your posts on a regular basis.

Today your connections are platform-based. In other words, you must connect with people uniquely on each platform you use. In the future, this will likely be seamless. Your connections will probably travel from platform to platform with you, and you'll have contact with them wherever, whenever, and however you desire. These connections form communities.

Communities

Whether the platform terms these groups, circles, networks, divisions, lists, or another term is irrelevant. Communities form around specific topics or groups of interest. You, the leader, your mission, organization, or vision may be that topic. Your competition could be that topic. Connections following your posts may be there for you—regardless of the subject matter in your posts. Alternatively, the community may form around a shared passion, such as Southern cooking.

Communities today vary from platform to platform. Some are more professional, others more personal in nature. In the future, the personal versus professional divide will probably be less obvious. Communities will also be more ubiquitous. It won't matter where a community was formed because the content and communication across that community will be seamless for connections.

Posts

Regardless of the medium you use, any piece of content shared among the community is a post. The cavemen posted drawings on the wall. Today we share many types of posts, including images, video, text, audio, and more. In the future, we may post holograms, Star-Trek era food replicator recipes, or other three-dimensional abstractions.

Mediums

"The medium is the message."[12] Well, for our purposes, the medium is the format of the post. This could be video, imagery, text, audio or any combination thereof. Early man used imagery, verbal tones, and gestures. Our medium in the future may include a replicator—at least, I hope so. The medium is the type of content within the post.

Ratings

We really can't make up our minds on this one. In fact, I bet ratings will be the last ageless concept we standardize on. In prehistoric days, the ratings were a series of hoots, grunts, and hollers—I doubt they counted them, though. Since then, we have evolved to use the terms likes, loves, stars, hearts, +1s, and more.

I don't know what we'll call them in the future or if we'll ever agree on one term, but in essence, ratings are how much praise or criticism an object receives in social media. That object could be just about anything: a post, company, person, connection, community, church, product, service, or just about anything that could be described.

Shares

Clubbing over the head and dragging someone into the cave to see the image may have sufficed for cavemen. Thankfully, we have evolved to reposts, shares, retweets, repins, or almost any posting term preceded by "re." This is the forwarding or distribution. It doesn't necessarily have to be repeated to be a share, but it often is.

In the future, sharing will also be seamless. With the decreasing personal versus professional divide, most of what you like will be public knowledge. Both as a leader and as a consumer, this will have major implications for how you, your products, and your services will be perceived.

Now, some of my technophile peers will critique this universal view of the social media space. They will suggest that the specific social media name, format, and technology do matter. They will say that exactly how the technology is used makes a difference in the tactics a person should pursue. They may be right—when it comes to tactics.

When it comes to leadership concepts and the principles in this book, though, the timeless concepts are what we need to understand. I would argue that these timeless concepts are the heart of social media for anyone to address, but that may be another book.

The point is that social media concepts do not become obsolete. The terminology and names we use will evolve. This is especially true if we speak in the context of a single platform. Here, I reference these timeless concepts to keep the concepts in the book equally timeless. Plus, you won't feel like you're reading a book that was written by a Neanderthal.

Social Media Summary
In this section, I first explored the common arguments against social media. It should now be clear that timeless concepts of social media are not just some fad. Instead, advances in digital communication technology have simply expanded what is possible. Next, I refuted the argument that social media lacks

an ROI. The reality is that social media provides a stronger ROI and greater measurability than previous media. The last common argument, that social media is a waste of time, was also refuted by describing the tools available in social media as often the most efficient means of communication. Yet I explained that traditional media still has value by inspiring the inquiry. Leaders today can use traditional media to inspire the interest of their stakeholders. The difference is that this is where traditional media's value now ends.

Next, I looked at how social media changes the way we work, play, and live. This was expressed through my short story about the ubiquitous nature of social media. Through this story and the changes explained earlier, I highlighted a massive power shift from the organization to the masses. This power shift has major implications for leaders. Because of this power shift, it's more critical than ever for leaders to serve all of their stakeholders. This is in contrast to the popular emphasis on single groups of shareholders as we saw in the industrial revolution.

Finally, I wrapped up this section on social media by explaining the principles of social media that survive the test of time. Whatever platform or medium you use, there are constant concepts like sharing, posting, rating, and so on. Rather than use platform-specific terminology or technology names that rapidly become outdated, I will use these technology-agnostic terms to explain our leadership principles.

Reflection
1. Why should you care about social media?
2. Who are the social media leaders in your organization today?
3. Is your organization ready for the future of social media?

LEADING PEOPLE

"People do not care how much you know until they know how much you care."

–John C. Maxwell

Leadership is about people. Lucky for modern leaders, so is social media. The best leaders today know how to use social media to have a more effective influence. This section is about leaders and the social media related to the people those leaders serve.

Leadership Communication Eras

Before the printing press, leadership was personal, but suffered the constraint of scale. Military power was the popular solution to achieving large capacity leadership. That form of leadership was about power and control.

Then the printing press arrived and enabled mass communication. This allowed leaders to spread direct communications far and wide, but in only one direction. Still the people had no way of communicating directly back to the leader.

Enter social media and the phase of mass dialogue leadership. Now the masses finally have a way to get their message heard by the leader. It may not be a single individual's precise wording, but the message is heard.

Leaders now find it more difficult than ever to deny feedback. As feedback is shared in social channels, communities see it, rate it, and elevate the most agreeable content. In the end, the message most strongly supported by the community is raised to the top.

To be certain, the leader still decides how to react to the feedback. As a result, there remain good and bad leaders. In fact, some of the best leaders must not capitulate to many requests. After all, leadership still means making tough calls that are unpopular at times.

As Rosalynn Carter said, "A leader takes people where they want to go. A great leader takes people where they don't necessarily want to go, but ought to be." It's still the mark of great leadership to sift the desires from the needs of the community and respond accordingly. Great leaders serve the needs first and desires second. As a result, what's popular may not be the best action.

Before social media, bad leaders could simply pretend that they did not hear the popular demands of people. Leaders who attempt a similar excuse today will be quickly disproved. This is because the community can clearly see the same communication, highlighted for the leader in popular forums. As a result, great leaders must respond to the community's requests. Whether they choose a path or not, great leaders must address the paths requested by the masses.

This is why dictatorial nations like China, Cuba, Iran, and North Korea try, often unsuccessfully, to block or censor social media usage. Their leaders remain in power not through granted authority, but because they control the masses and prevent popular sentiment uprising. This is also why so much of the success in the Arab Spring is attributed to social media tools.[14]

You now have a choice: participate in the mass dialogue or ignore it. One is the path of democracy, the other, dictatorship.

Successful leadership in the social media revolution means more personal leadership. Leaders who represent the values of their community will stand on their own authority, not beneath the veil of control.

Personal Leadership Examples

Without looking, who is the publisher of this book? My guess is you didn't know without looking. I certainly never noticed this attribute of my books before I met Michael Hyatt, then CEO of Thomas Nelson Publishers.

Michael Hyatt

Michael Hyatt was the CEO and Chairman of the Board for Thomas Nelson Publishers, the largest Christian publisher and among the largest trade publishers in the world. I'd never heard of the company. As I said before, I had never cared who published my books.

I stumbled upon Michael Hyatt before his blog hit mega-status. At the time, he was certainly best known for his career in publishing. Now he's probably best known for his social media thought leadership, and book on the same topic: *Platform: Get Noticed in a Noisy World.*[15]

What attracted me to Michael was not his status as CEO or his interest in social media per se. Those items piqued my interest, but what really got me hooked as a follower was his personal style. Michael was incredibly responsive. I posted a comment to him and got an almost immediate response.

Months later, I mentioned him in a post on my own site. Within minutes, he'd commented on the post, thanking me. It impressed me how on top of his community he was. He was aware of posts the moment they appeared, read them immediately, and responded with clear interest.

And so it continued for months. I absorbed all I could about Michael's perspectives on leadership and social media. After occasionally mentioning him in my own material or commenting to him directly, I'd always get direct feedback from him—almost immediately.

You might be thinking, "Who has the time to be that responsive?" But remember that most of these comments were short post formats, 140 characters or fewer, often completed while standing in line somewhere. You might also think, "Yeah, but to thousands of followers?" But remember that I did offer some benefit.

I was compiling feedback for Michael and generating content that referenced him and his work. I was essentially free advertising for him and Thomas Nelson.

This doesn't mean he was only replying to me because I had something to offer. It means that everybody has something of value to offer.

The relationship you build with your followers—one or two posts at a time—is an investment from which you will reap returns tenfold. Is it easy? Of course not. This is no magic pill—nor is there ever going to be one – but it does help.

Yet Michael had that touch. He listened to his readers and subscribers. He responded to them and garnered their input, adapting his work to be of the greatest benefit to his followers as he went. His book *Platform* is a testament to this.

Just because a leader is on social media platforms does not mean they are effective at connecting with people. For example, in contrast to Michael, Roger Goodell failed to provide a personal leadership touch on social media platforms.

Roger Goodell

The next two examples come to us both from Amy Jo Martin's Digital Royalty team and her book, *Renegades Write the Rules*.[16] In it, she offers a terrific example of how social media, when done right, can make leadership personal again. But first, she begins by showing us an example of a missed opportunity in the NFL's infamous Roger Goodell.

Goodell is the National Football League's commissioner which is essentially the CEO of the entire league. As such, his leadership decisions are often disputed, and he's performed his fair share of questionable actions. You'd think social media is the perfect opportunity for Goodell to tell his side of the story directly to the fans.

As many leaders do today, though, Roger Goodell entered the social media scene by dipping his toes in the water to see if it was warm. While he did find it warm enough, he then decided that getting wet, swimming in the water, then drying off and changing clothes was not for him. So he paid somebody else to do it for him.

In her book, Martin explains how Goodell's social media account, used essentially as another formal Public Relations channel, did more harm than good:

> "Then the looming (NFL) Lockout in 2010 heated up and Goodell's (social) account went dark. He went completely missing for months . . . What message did Goodell's sudden silence send? For starters, it confirmed that his following wasn't very important to him in the first place. He'd taken the stage, dimmed the lights and then turned his back on the audience."

When you enter the social media circuit, you expose yourself for who you are. This happens through action and, in Goodell's case, inaction. When you choose not to be personal, you're actually telling everyone something about your personality: you don't want to share it. In most cases, when left to their own assumptions, your audience will assume you have something to hide.

Dana White

Now contrast Roger Goodell to Dana White, one of the owners of the mixed martial arts league, Ultimate Fighting Championship (UFC). Five years ago, most people had never heard of the UFC. Today, it produces more than thirty live events, and its programming is available in over 354 million homes in more than 145 countries and in 19 languages. In her book, Amy Jo Martin attributes the explosive growth of UFC to "major social media exposure that gives fans real-time connections with not only the individual fighters, but also one of its founders."

When Dana White considered entering the social media scene, he reached out to Amy Jo Martin. Martin took the meeting to discuss social media opportunities for the UFC. She recounts their first meeting:

> Dana: "Listen, fans don't give a f*ck about what I do all day . . . it's boring sh*t."
>
> Amy Jo: "They *do* care and it's not boring . . . What did you do just before this meeting?"
>
> Dana: "I reviewed T-Shirt designs and they sucked. I told my creative team to try again."
>
> Amy Jo: "What if you took a photo of the designs and asked UFC fans—the people who are buying the (darn) things, what they think of these designs? Wouldn't that be easier than guessing what they like?"

Amy Jo notes that Dana is "incapable of faking anything." She goes on to say, "He is who he is across any communication medium and that's a perfect recipe for social media success, if your audience values what you bring to the table." In short, Dana White was the "perfect fit to humanize the UFC brand with its fans."

There are many great stories about how Dana White connects directly and very personally with fans, in a style that is naturally his own. Like the time he told off a detractor or how he posts locations he'll be at to hand out free tickets to lucky fans. He's also known to share details about his personal conversations with fighters just hours before their bouts. But probably the best example of how Dana used his personal style to evoke leadership and influence from fans was the time he mistakenly shared his office number on social media.

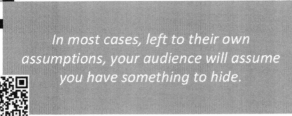

While attempting to help a fan out, Dana mistakenly posted his direct phone line to all (one and a half million) connections. Within minutes, at least nine million people had his direct office phone number. This didn't faze the UFC leader. To borrow another sporting term, he stepped up to the plate, took accountability, and turned a screw ball into a home run:

> *"Well, if I'm stupid enough to tweet my phone number to everyone, I'm going to take their calls."*
> —Dana White

And take them he did. He took as many calls as possible immediately afterward. More importantly, he set up a program for fan calls that would continue indefinitely. The UFC then extended that program, setting up "fan phones" with UFC fighters. This allowed unprecedented direct access for fans to their sports stars. Through a partnership with a mobile phone provider, fighters invite fans via social media to call them and the fans love it. Every so often a fighter will post that they are available to take phone calls from fans. Not all fans make it through to speak with the fighters. However, those who do, share what they discussed, and the rest of the fans eat it up.

What other sport has such a direct access line for fans? More importantly, it enables fans of the sport to see directly into the personality of the leaders in the sport.

Martin summed it up well, after assessing the great impact Dana's role in social media has had on the UFC brand, when she said, "So much for the notion that exposure at the executive level is bad for business."

But, like Goodell, what if leaders make an appearance and fail to sustain that presence? Once you're in, are you all in forever?

Too Big to be Personal?

I mentioned how fond I am of Michael Hyatt and his ability to be very personal. That comes with a postscript to say that he's changed a bit as of late. He's still the same great, personable guy. However, after leaving his CEO role at Thomas Nelson and throwing himself full time into his own business (speaking, writing, and mentoring others), it's clear that he has less time to invest in his personal interactions.

Michael's blog also hit mega-blogger status, diminishing the perceived value in each subscriber's contribution back to the site.

When I first started following Michael, I was typically among his top commenters each month. Now, I rarely comment, in part because, by the time I do, there are already hundreds of comments. At that point, I'm certain someone has already said what I would, and I'm not going to read through hundreds of comments to ensure mine is not a repeat.

Has Michael gotten too big to be personal? Perhaps. But at the same time, he's also set a great example on mitigating this perception.

From One to Many to Community

Mike saw the implications of his success. He could no longer be the only one directly addressing comments. He needed help, and he knew that he had some great people he could count on. These included many of his largest commenters to date. So he turned his site from a blog only, which emphasized a one-to-many relationship, into a community which emphasized a many-to-many relationship. How?

Mike recruited community leaders. These individuals are tasked with reading and responding to hundreds of comments he receives on each post. If the community leader sees something special that Michael should respond to, they highlight it for him. This enables Michael to remain directly engaged with subscribers, while freeing him up to conduct the other necessary aspects of his business.

Of course, Michael still remains engaged even when his community leaders are not. I still get the occasional unsolicited comment, post, or other feedback from him. It's not the same, but he's reaching literally thousands more people. Given his excellent content and influence on the betterment of leadership everywhere, I'm okay with that.

As a leader, you may reach a point like Michael did and find yourself unable to handle the flood of requests alone. This is a good thing. It means your mission is catching on to a larger support base.

Still, you will find yourself flustered—disappointed you can no longer respond directly to every request. Congratulations, you've been elevated from individual contributor in your mission to team leader. It's time to select and coach your team, as Michael Hyatt did.

Whether you lead alone or coach a team, you must maintain transparency. Any attempt to mask reality could be construed as a veneer identity, and these will no longer survive.

Death of the Veneer Identity

Amy Jo Martin also coined the term and analogy of veneer identities in her book. The term veneer refers to a thin layer of substance on top of the real product. Two of the most common traditional veneers are dental and wood veneers. Dental veneers are a thin, artificial coating over a less attractive or weakened tooth. In carpentry, a wood veneer is a thin layer of finer-looking, artificial wood on top of a lower-grade quality, composite, or cheaper wood.

In both cases, the veneer is an artificial layer, masking the reality underneath. The underlying reality is something the owner does not want exposed to others. Over time, these artificial layers wear down and fall apart much more quickly than the real thing.

For centuries, leaders and organizations were able to uphold such veneers to their identity.

Corporate Veneers

Organizations masked the realities inside by plastering Public Relations material that claimed outstanding ethics, morals, and interest in their people and consumers. The reality may have been a singular focus on the investor, selling low quality goods while overextending employees. However, to the outside world, the only message was often what they could find in print or on the company website.

Leadership Veneers

Leaders pretended to be exemplary champions of the people, speaking proudly of how they treat others in the public square. Behind closed doors, however, employees of these leaders received frequent tongue-lashings and rapidly decreasing benefits. Yet prospective new employees and the rest of the outside world knew little of the reality behind the smoke and mirrors.

In both cases, there were limited opportunities for exposing the reality of coarser material beneath the surface. After all, how would a prospective employee really know the company's culture? How would a recruiter considering an applicant know the reality of that leader's behavior? Thankfully, this has changed. The veneer identity has met its demise—a death we've long awaited.

R.I.P. Corporate Veneers

Want to bury the real culture of your company's backstabbing politics and singular focus on the investor? Good luck. Now there are countless forums for prospective employees and consumers to see beneath the surface. Some examples:

> **Best and Worst Places to Work**: Websites specifically focused at reviewing employers release best and worst employer lists, based upon actual employee feedback.[17]

> **Connections**: Potential employees, analysts, and reporters can find connections inside your organization. These could be advocates or detractors. It is very easy to connect over three degrees of separation or more.

R.I.P. Leadership Veneers

Thanks to social media, people expect authentic and transparent leadership. One study found that eighty-two percent of employees trust a company more when the CEO and leadership team communicate via social media.[18] There are many reasons for this, including the removal of the veneer. Employees no longer see only the public mask, but the internal struggles as well. Is the executive a family man? Does the leader struggle with the challenge of being a working mother? Does the person have a strong faith or other moral and ethical convictions? All this, when done right, resonates with employees and other connections. The executive who does not utilize social media will find it more difficult to build support and a following.

Thankfully, the time has come to bury corporate and leadership veneers. Will there still be some roaming the earth? Of course, but like their walking dead counterpart—the zombie—these identities will meander aimlessly with less and less support. Like the dental and wood veneers before them, support for these leaders will degrade and quickly expose the underlying weaknesses. After all, nobody really gets to know a zombie.

> *The veneer identity has met its demise—a death we've long awaited.*

The Role of Knowing Someone

The leader doesn't have to know the follower, but the follower must know the leader. This is the simple reality of our new world. Barack Obama can't possibly know the thirty-one million followers he has on just one social media platform.[13] Yet there is no doubt that many of those followers believe they know *him*. Why is that? Because people see his life. Barack shares his personal life a bit more openly than many presidents before him, though I admit some shared more than we cared to know . . .

People follow those they know. I want to help Michael Hyatt, Amy Jo Martin, Chris Brogan, Joe Iarrocie, Jack King, Larry Spears, Paul Gillin, and countless other individuals whom I follow on social media. Not because they're my best friends or have anything to offer me. Instead, I want to help them because I know them. I know what they stand for and how they influence trends, actions, and other individuals. I know these people are servant leaders who advocate principles similar to my own.

Social media enables this. Because people share more about themselves, their principles, and their lives, we know them more than we've known leaders in previous generations. This brings us, as their supporters, closer to them. By investing in social media, leaders can strengthen support, advocacy, and influence.

The Role of Trust

Social media provides the opportunity for leaders to increase the trust that their connections have in them and that they have in their connections. In *The Speed of Trust: The One Thing That Changes Everything*, author Stephen M. R. Covey explains that trust has a significant impact on cost and speed for any organization:[19]

Speed

High-trust environments operate faster than low-trust organizations. For example, if people trust their leader, they will respond to requests quickly. If they do not trust a leader, time is wasted while they second-guess, research the background for requests, and spend time gossiping about intentions.

Cost

The implications of speed incur cost increases or decreases. Teams that react more quickly save money. Teams that take longer to respond and deliver results cost more.

Building Trust

Covey explains that high-trust environments benefit from a trust "dividend." Social media offers a terrific opportunity to build and increase trust dividends. Leaders who leverage social media to share their intentions and logic behind key decisions build quicker support. In one-on-one meetings, a leader may explain the background for critical decisions, but anyone not present is left to question the intent.

> *Social media offers a terrific opportunity to build and increase trust dividends.*

Once published in an easily shareable fashion on social channels, that same logic is amplified. Likewise, leaders who publish beliefs and intentions—and then stick to them—provide a constant record for followers to reference. Trust builds upon trust, amplifying its own effect exponentially.

Destroying Trust

Of course, as easily as leaders can build trust with social media, they can also lose it. Covey refers to the costs that stem from a lack of trust as trust "taxes." These trust taxes arise in social media when leaders fail to do what they say.

Once a leader commits to something in a public forum like social media, then fails to follow through, trust is lost. A tax is incurred.

I know that, reading this, some of you will say that's why you fear social media. A leader must be able to shift priorities in changing circumstances. But that's the beauty of social media. The same platform can be used to explain, in new posts, why the leader did not deliver as promised. If a leader does not have sound reason for their failure, they have a leadership problem, not a social media problem.

According to Covey, there are five types of trust:

1. Self Trust
2. Relationship Trust
3. Organizational Trust
4. Market Trust
5. Societal Trust (Contribution)

1. Self Trust

> *"Trust yourself, then you will know how to live."*
> —*Johann Wolfgang von Goethe*

To have self trust, a leader must trust herself and believe she is someone others can trust. This is achieved through integrity and results.

Integrity is reinforced by commitments, documenting what you say. Bloggers often say they blog as much for themselves as anyone else—it helps them put their thoughts and intentions in writing. This increases the accountability for the blogger by exposing their beliefs, intentions, and perspectives to the world. It's much harder to change your perspective when you've proclaimed it and left it for the world to record and recall any time. If there is not logic to support that change, followers will be confused, and your influence will be weakened.

The same holds true for any social media participation. It may be anything, from something as simple as your favorite sports team to a subject as complicated as your religious beliefs. If you proclaim this year that you're a fan of the Philadelphia football team and bash the Dallas team, then next year praise Dallas and bash Philly, your followers and subscribers will challenge your credibility. Likewise, if you proclaim transubstantiation during the Eucharist one year, but the next year you say communion reflects only a symbolic representation of the body and blood, how seriously can your congregation take you?

This also extends from the personal to the professional. A leader who waffles on personal topics will lose credibility in professional topics as well. For instance, if you waffle on your sports fanaticism, your stakeholders will make that subconscious leap to your professional stance as well: "Will she really stick to her decisions on the strategic direction for the company? After all, she's not consistent in other areas."

As leaders share their intent online and connections reflect on their results, they build self trust. This transparency in front of the community forces a leader to solidify his or her beliefs. Before posting a decision, the leader must consider the arguments that will come from the community. When these arguments are considered, the leader solidifies their decision. The documentation of that decision and the results of the decision are observed by the community. The community, in turn, holds the leader accountable. When done right, transparently and completely, the leader's confidence and trust in self grows through this process.

Your results and credibility drive self trust. This is the foundation for all other trust and therefore the first wave. Once you have self trust, you begin to build relationship trust.

2. Relationship Trust
"Men trust their ears less than their eyes."—Herodotus

Relationship trust is about the trust stakeholders have in you. You build this trust by paying the trust dividends into the accounts of others. In other words, you build the trust others have in you by demonstrating trustworthy behaviors. There are thirteen of these trustworthy, relationship trust building behaviors in Covey's book. However, the five greatest opportunities among these behaviors for leaders in social media are:

1. **Talk Straight**: Be clear and concise, but thorough. People want leaders who don't mix words and confuse issues. The power of social media tools to share clear, concise, yet powerful and thorough messages to a broad community is unmatched.

2. **Create Transparency**: Breaking down the barriers and intermediaries of messages between you and stakeholders increases transparency. The more genuine and candid you are on social media, the stronger your relationship trust.

3. **Deliver Results**: Results matter. Sharing your results with the community and connecting those results to prior commitments builds trust. Before social media, you had to rely on others to do this for you. Now, you can share these results directly with stakeholders.

4. **Practice Accountability**: There are many great examples of leaders taking accountability in social media. You'll hear about how Domino's Pizza did this later. For now, just know that leaders can use the public forum of social media to hold themselves and others accountable.

5. **Listen First**: A key factor in social media success is the ability to listen to your stakeholders. Social media enables and empowers leaders to know their stakeholders and what matters to them, better than ever before. Leverage this opportunity to listen to what your people are saying.

These behaviors will strengthen the relationship trust you have with your connections. Social media offers the platform on which to maximize these five behaviors. As you build your relationship trust, it builds into the next wave: Organizational Trust.

3. Organizational Trust

> *"Politics is war without bloodshed while war is politics with bloodshed."*—Mao Tse-Tung

Dirty politics, backstabbing, and other bad corporate behaviors are symptoms of failing organizational trust. When trust throughout the organization fails, it causes systemic breakdowns in efficiency. Worse, it makes the company a horrible place to work. When employees don't enjoy work, they leave their best performance at the door.

So how does a leader drive good organizational trust? You align the organization on the *practice* of common values and principles. Practice is emphasized because just writing them down is not sufficient. You need to catch people practicing these values and share them publicly. Social media makes this easier than ever before. For example, a leader who sees an employee practicing a value of "helping others" can snap a photo and post it to the community.

Through a mass dialogue, rather than a massive one-way communication, leaders can also hear the challenges and concerns of the community. The leader can then address the matters directly. Internal social media solutions, often delivered through "collaboration software," are excellent solutions for alignment. These collaboration software packages enable social media solutions that are internal to the organization, without fear of releasing sensitive information.

You want to encourage open communication, constructive criticism, and other positive behaviors that help strengthen and improve your performance. At the same time, there are factors you may not want to share externally: concerns like competitive analysis and product innovations. Internal collaboration suites enable the mass dialogue within the company.

Leaders need to drive alignment across the organization. Alignment occurs when stakeholders and leaders are engaged in a mass dialogue. Once this happens, you can build the fourth wave: Market Trust.

Alignment occurs when stakeholders and leaders are engaged in a mass dialogue.

Bad Guys are Good for Alignment

As you address your organization's alignment, consider: who is your "bad guy"? In for-profits, it's likely your toughest competitor or the one with the least ethical practices. In non-profits, it's the problem you seek to solve, like hunger, disease, or educational inequality. In religion, perhaps Satan. Whoever or whatever your bad guy is, make sure the organization knows it by frequently and regularly referring back to it. In the absence of an external bad guy, the organization finds one internally. This results in dirty politics, backstabbing, and other behaviors that destroy alignment.

4. Market Trust

> *"Character is like a tree and reputation like a shadow. The shadow is what we think of it; the tree is the real thing."—Abraham Lincoln*

Your brand is your reputation. If you're in a for-profit, you may have several brands you manage. If you're an independent, you have a personal brand.

What is the reputation you have with stakeholders? This is your Market Trust.

Social media is full of branding case studies—good and bad—where brand reputations are boosted or leveled in a matter of hours. These occur whether the brand leadership is present or not in the discussion. That said, the majority of positive incidents and avoided potential disasters occur when brand leadership *is* present in the dialogue.

Influencing market trust is among the greatest opportunities of social media. Perception is reality until it is changed. When a fact is misrepresented, leaders can quickly engage and rectify the situation.

If a politician chooses not to endorse an environmental protection act, the community may perceive him as too aligned with big business. However, if that politician engages in the dialogue and explains the negative impact the act would have on local employment, it may change the community's perception. To do this, the leader may create a post that explains the negative side of the act and underscore his intent. Then, as readers respond, support, and critique his logic, the leader remains engaged in the discussion. Very quickly, the community can more fully understand the leader's intent.

To influence market trust, listen carefully to the community surrounding your brand and engage with stakeholders and influencers to ensure that reality is understood. The strength of your Market Trust will lead to the strength of the fifth and final wave we cover: Societal Trust.

5. Societal Trust

> *"It is not what we get. But who we become, what we contribute . . . that gives meaning to our lives."—Tony Robbins*

One of the greatest detractors of trust in our society is the greed and self-centeredness of organizations like Enron and individuals like Bernie Madoff.[20] People trust leaders who seek to contribute to the benefit of stakeholders, rather than take away from them. This is one reason why Servant Leadership principles are in demand (see the "Your Principles" section). Those who serve stakeholders first are trusted more because they contribute to the benefit and growth of others.

But it's not altruistic. It's reality. You don't have to be poor and give away every penny without compensation to achieve societal trust. For example, Bill Gates came under a great deal of fire for taking too much early in his career and later balanced this perception with his foundation work. Other individuals with high societal trust based on their contributions to society include Oprah Winfrey and Bono—neither suffering in despair.

The point of social media is to consider what you share. More specifically, consider who benefits from what you share. If ninety percent of what you share is pure advertising for you, your products, or your services, you're not contributing. Instead, make sure the majority of what you share is targeted at helping your stakeholders. It's okay to advertise once in a while, just be clear about it and ensure that it is a small percentage of your mass dialogue.

Contribution Ratio

In their book, *Trust Agents: Using the Web to Build Influence, Improve Reputation, and Earn Trust,"*[21] authors Chris Brogan and Julien Smith suggest a ratio of twelve to one, focusing on yourself (with self-promotion or advertising) one time for every twelve times you focus on stakeholders. Others have since suggested similar concepts at a higher ratio, such as twenty to one. Whatever ratio works for you, ensure that the majority of your dialogue focuses on serving stakeholders more, and yourself less.

Trust is no longer a perk; it's a basic requirement. Stakeholders won't even buy a ticket for entry, let alone participate in the mission, if they do not have trust in the leader. Leaders can leverage social media to create, strengthen, and extend trust with stakeholders.

Leading People Summary

For centuries, mass communication meant a message in a single direction. Finally, mass communication is personal. Advances in technology enable leaders to have a mass dialogue for the first time in history. In this section, I presented three examples of leaders who use or abuse this opportunity.

> *Trust is no longer a perk; it's a basic requirement.*

Michael Hyatt did a fantastic job, grew a massive following, faced the challenges this growth introduced and found a solution by building a community. Roger Goodell, unfortunately, missed this opportunity by introducing himself to the social media stage then turning his back on stakeholders at the most important moment. Finally, never one to turn away from difficult situations, Dana White showed us how strong personalities can make a huge impact for organizations they lead. Dana made this impact by being himself, whom fans loved, in social media.

Next I walked you through how social media killed the veneer identity for leaders. In ages past, leaders could say one thing and do another. Much like dental and wood veneers, which mask the reality of a less valuable interior, leadership veneers were artificial and weak. Social media exposes the leadership veneer. As a result, leaders can no longer sustain such a façade.

I wrapped up this People Leadership section by studying the importance and types of trust. Based on Stephen M. R. Covey's work, we explained the five waves of trust for leaders and its applicability to social media. Each wave builds up the next and social media offers terrific opportunities within each wave. These waves included Self Trust, Relationship Trust, Organizational Trust, Market Trust and Societal Trust.

Yes, leadership is about the people. Communication technology advances that enable social media also enable leaders to connect directly with more people than ever before. But to do so, you need a platform. I'll cover your platform in the next section.

Reflection
1. How are you using social media to be more personal with your stakeholders?
2. Does your organization have a culture you're proud of, or is it hidden under a veneer?
3. What is the degree of trust you and your organization have in each wave of trust?

YOUR PLATFORM

Ideas are cheap; it's the execution that matters. Regardless of how great your idea is, you need people who buy in and the support of others to make real change take place. Your platform helps you do that. Publishing is a great way to build that platform.

Traditional Publishing Model

The traditional publishing model placed control of great ideas in the hands of big publishing companies. From the time of Gutenberg, he who owned the press controlled the message. If you wanted your thoughts published, you had to convince the press owner (publisher) that it was worth printing. Of course, money played a role. You could also convince investors and pay the publisher to get your idea out.

Fast-forward several centuries, and not much had changed. In fact, agents, the middlemen, were needed to navigate the publishing waters and to get your idea considered by publishers. Most authors who approached a publisher would be quickly turned away and told to first find an agent instead. That is, until the evolution of digital social media.

Before modern social media, the publishing companies still controlled the fate of many ideas. While most traditional publishers still prefer to work with agents, there are alternative publishing channels available in social media platforms.

New Publishing Model

As a result of social media, two major changes have been made to the publishing model:

1. Anyone can publish their ideas.
2. Major publishers require a platform.

Now, anyone can publish their ideas in multiple formats. The question is a matter of reach and scale. Many leaders want to reach a broad audience with their message. One way to reach such a broad audience is through traditional print publishers, who help place books in new markets. These new markets mean new readers and therefore a broader influence. The problem is that major publishers want the author or leader to have a platform first. So many leaders, seeking to publish their message, begin to build a digital platform to gain the interest of traditional publishers.

Anyone Can Publish

As a leader, you can create and build a digital platform to publish your ideas. Through technology, it is easier than ever for leaders to publish their vision. Formats include blogs, podcasts, eBooks, audiobooks, and more. All of these publishing options, as well as traditional hard copies, can be produced at very low costs. In fact, many publishing options can be executed at no cost. In short, any audience with access to technology can be reached via a self-publishing model.

No longer must an author get approval from strangers to distribute his or her ideas to the world. This is fantastic news for leaders who seek to expand their influence.

Of course, this self-publishing opportunity presents a challenge as well. Namely, the space is crowded. According to Google's Executive Chairman, Eric Schmidt, we now create as much content every two days as we created in the entirety of history until 2003.[22]

In a space that crowded, there is a lot of noise, and few are heard. If that's true, how in the world are you going to get your ideas consumed and supported? The answer is simple: a platform.

Publishers Want a Platform

Chances are you've got some great ideas in your head. Ideas that could change the world—or at least your corner of it.

You have so many ideas that you could write a book. In fact, let's say you do write a book. Now you want to reach a broad audience.

You've heard about self-publishing, but you also know the big publishing houses are your best chance at quickly reaching a big audience. You want to serve that larger community, so you pursue the more traditional publishing route. You decide to look for a book agent.

You quickly find that this is not easy. Agent after agent turns you down or, worse, ignores your proposal. Going directly to publishers does not work either.

You don't understand. Your idea is great, and you're confident in your writing skills. Why will nobody take you on? Finally, a kind agent takes the time to explain why they decline to represent you:

> You have no platform.

Wait, what? Isn't that what they're supposed to help you build? Not anymore. This reminds me of a scene from the pseudo-classic, 1987 business flick, *Secret of My Success*.[23] In the scene, recent college graduate Brantley Foster (played by Michael J. Fox) is struggling to find work in New York City. His interviewer is about to turn him down for the position.

> **Interviewer**: I'm sorry, Mr. Foster. We need someone with experience.
> **Foster**: But how can I get experience until I get a job that gives me experience?
> **Interviewer**: If we gave you a job, just to give you experience . . . you'd take that experience and get a better job. Then that experience would benefit someone else.

Replace "experience" with "a platform" and "job" with "a book," and you have the same dilemma. Agents today explain that the publishing space is so crowded that it's more and more expensive to adequately market a book. As a result, publishers want to know what you will do to market the book yourself.

How will you, personally and directly, drive sales? This minimizes the risk to the publisher and increases their return on investment. Furthermore, there are thousands of bloggers, podcasters, and other thought-leaders who have a platform already. Why should they take on an author without a platform?

Of course, the irony is that, once you have a platform, you need a traditional publisher less to get your idea heard. This is why more and more authors and leaders are choosing the path of self-publishing. Once you have a platform, you have your own connections. With your own connections, the dependency upon a traditional publisher decreases. So what exactly is a platform?

The Leader's Platform

Historically, platforms were used by speakers to reach a broader audience. Kings shouted from balconies of the castle, so that they could be heard by their people. Priests spoke from pulpits to be seen and heard by congregants. Rebels did the same, grabbing a wooden stand or other raised surface to be seen above the crowd. Whatever the origin or message, platforms helped a message be received by a broader audience.

The original platforms were physical structures that served to lift the speaker above the crowd. Today, and for the purposes of this book, a platform is any tool of a similar purpose. Most often today though, the platform refers to a digital platform. With digital platforms, the capabilities, reach, and power are more extensive.

Platform Models

Today, we have many different models for our platform—some better than others. However, most digital platforms fit into one of three models.

Stronghold

The term "stronghold" originally defined a physical fortress, built to protect and defend the people and ideals contained within. Those within the fortress held ideals in contrast to those outside the fortification walls. The expansion of those ideals and messages required a major investment. For example, in order to expand a leader's influence, military power was often used to conquer neighboring fortresses.

A digital stronghold is similar. Leaders often develop their centralized message or theme within the company walls on a corporate intranet. You may create a blog, website, or other single instance where you create and share ideas within a defined space. This is a starting point. You need a compilation of ideas, a foundation upon which you can grow and share interest with like-minded individuals.

Expansion

Stronghold marketing is needed to build the stronghold platform. The attack on a new market or community is made with massive investments in multiple media forums. For example, to attack a new community, marketers buy disruption-based, push advertising. Examples of disruption-based advertising include television ads, print ads, and similar traditional advertisements. These advertisements are nothing more than distractions from what the community really wants to see. This expands the platform at a high cost. While a single advertisement may suffice, more often the consumer is "conquered" only after a barrage of advertisements.

The same is true for expanding leadership influence in this model. You act as the marketer does in this regard. A heavy investment is required to expand that influence from fortress to fortress. As a result, leaders with stronghold model fortresses often find the effort to build and sustain that platform too difficult. The result is that many leaders who use the stronghold model platform abandon their efforts before they take hold.

An example of building and expanding a stronghold platform may begin with a secured blog. The leader creates a mission and publishes many posts. However, only registered and authorized users can see this content. As a next step, the leader creates a community on his or her favorite video-sharing website. However, like the blog site, only registered and authorized users can see this content.

Figure 1: Stronghold platform model

Because the two sites are not directly linked, the leader must create separate content on each site: videos are posted on the video site and blog posts on the blog. There is no direct connection, and only authorized users can see posts on either site. This is the stronghold platform model across two different websites: the blog and the video-sharing sites.

While the stronghold platform model is expensive to expand, it is often the starting point for leaders. Within the safety and comfort of a stronghold, leaders can develop their ideas, content, and assets that provide value to their followers— both current and prospective. This can be done with minimal distraction from naysayers and with limited overhead investment.

Spider Web Model

Spiders use a web to catch traffic. A web, spread across the right space and at the right angle, catches traffic passing by that sticks to a single point in the web. To reach its catch, the spider must move back and forth constantly across the web. The same is true of a spider web platform model.

Leaders building a spider web platform maintain a presence for their message on many different forums. For example, they may be updating posts and content on a dozen different websites. They must then check in regularly on all these sites to meet, update, and sustain captured traffic. If they are not constantly shuffling sites and redistributing messages, the leader and her team will quickly lose their base support. As a result, this model is also expensive.

Expansion

Expanding the spider web model requires exponential investments. Duplication of accounts, infrastructure, and content is necessary to add new sites. As the spider must spin and repair broken strands, so must the leader create and reinforce connections. The leader must constantly travel back-and-forth from one digital platform to another, maintaining many repositories.

Unlike the stronghold model, the spider web model is less disruptive. The leader often uses existing platforms, where the connections already exist. As a result, the switching cost is less. This switching cost refers to the effort required for connections to switch to your content, mission, or organization. Because your connection is already on the platforms where you reach them, the effort is little for them to join. Therefore, the spider web platform model is better than the stronghold platform model.

A leader building and expanding a spider web model platform may begin with a blog as well. However, the leader then expands to a favorite video-sharing site. Neither site requires registration, so it's not a stronghold. However, the leader keeps videos on the video site and text posts on the blog.

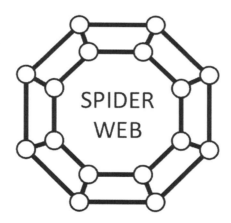

Figure 2: Spider Web platform model

As time passes, the leader begins to create many graphics. Fond of infographics (images used to relay detailed information), the leader begins posting a series of infographics on a section of yet another platform—the popular image-sharing site. All three sites reference each other: the video-sharing site references content on the image-sharing site, which references content on the blog, etc. However, no single site is used to house all of the content. As a result, the leader and her audience must spend time on many sites in order to consume all of the relevant content.

Another common starting point for platform-building leaders is this spider web model. Individuals with personal networks across several websites or other leaders' platforms begin to expand those bases and quickly find themselves regularly updating content and relationships on many sites.

Hub and Spoke Model

If the stronghold and spider web models are resource intensive, what is a better model? The hub and spoke model, of course. In essence, this approach combines the two previous models while removing the protective barriers of the stronghold and focusing more on integration with other sites than on duplication of content and networks.

In the hub and spoke platform model, the leader builds a strong home base at the center of the wheel. This may be a stronghold they have already created. The leader pulls their connections back to this central location where they store the bulk of their content, messaging, and valuable assets. It is the center of activity and where all roads on the platform lead. The spokes lead to other hubs or platforms. So the tip of each spoke may be another social network, another organization, a conference, some other form of network, or even a sub-hub.

In the hub and spoke platform model, leaders build their center of operations on one digital platform. This is often a blog, a social media site, their own website, or a corporate intranet. Then the posts from that hub are shared on other hubs or platforms. This sharing comprises the spokes.

Expansion

Expansion of the hub and spoke model is really about expanding the hub first. Extending from the hub's center point are many spokes: bi-directional roads to and from other sites, platforms, and networks. The point is to not make stops along the way and to not replicate the content on these other networks, but to engage in dialogue at the tips of the spokes. There, the leader must still provide value, but ultimately point interested parties back to the hub. The number of spokes or extension sites is limitless in this model. As the spokes grow, so should the hub, based on the traffic back to this central point.

Here's how an example of the hub and spoke model might work over time: A leader begins with a stronghold, by creating a blog. At first, users must register to join and read the content. During this time, it's mostly friends and family reading her content, while the leader fleshes out her mission statement, vision, and plan for the organization.

While she builds the content in the stronghold, she also begins engaging users on other platforms. This engagement may be commenting on posts that represent similar values to those she's building in her stronghold.

The leader then creates small communities formulated around similar ideals on other platforms. She begins to identify potential recruits and engages them in a dialogue. She identifies these individuals as they post like-minded content on image-sharing, video-sharing, or other social media websites. The dialogue may be about their content or snippets of shared content from posts in the leader's stronghold.

The shared posts resonate with her target audience on other platforms, and they begin to like, follow, and positively rate the leader and her content. In parallel to her stronghold, the leader is now building a spider web platform with content and communities across several other platforms.

As her content and connections grow, the leader removes the registration barrier to her stronghold. She then begins attracting connections from the spider web she created back to her former stronghold. Now that registration is no longer required, the barrier is removed, making her stronghold a hub. Because she's enticing connections back from the spider web platform, she's incorporated them into her spokes. As a result, the leader has effectively merged a stronghold platform and a separate spider web platform into a single hub and spoke platform.

Figure 3: Hub and Spoke platform model

Leaders can begin with either a stronghold platform or a spider web platform. Then the leader can merge the two, lower the barrier, and concentrate on strengthening feeds from spider web extensions. The hub and spoke platform captures a breadth of connections across the spokes and a depth of content in the hub. Leaders should create a strong value at the hub of their network and extend their reach across the spokes. The value at the hub is typically your core message, content, documentation, books, or other assets. The reach is extended across the spokes by sharing portions of that value and directing stakeholders back to the hub.

> *Leaders should create strong value at the hub of their network and extend their reach across the spokes.*

Value of a Platform

Consider your platform like real estate. The age-old adage of "location, location, location" is only half of the equation. It's also about leverage and reach. Yes, location is important. When it comes to social media, this means meeting your stakeholders where they are, rather than requiring them to come to you. In real estate, it's the same: the location of a retail outlet must be in the path of significant traffic, or sales flounder and value is diminished. Where leverage and reach come into play is in expanding that value.

Leverage

If McDonald's could reach all of its consumers from a single store, do you think they would still invest in all those locations? Or would the world's largest food chain invest in maximizing the profitability of a single location instead?

Given the choice of creating additional overhead at thousands of locations or maximizing profits through a single location, the decision seems obvious. Yet this is the decision leaders in the social media revolution face: invest equally in tons of locations or maximize your leverage through a primary location.

Sure, you still have to establish and maintain those outlet stores. The reason why the food chain has so many restaurant locations is the same reason that other platforms require their own kind of spokes: to meet their consumers where they are.

Yet at the same time, McDonald's doesn't duplicate the corporate office at every location. There's no need for each store to have its own Marketing, Public Relations, Accounting,

Finance, Legal, and Human Resource departments. Instead, each franchise leverages the investment and content of headquarters to benefit the individual spokes.

Effective leaders in social media leverage their platform to maximize its benefits in a similar fashion. Like the corporate headquarters, the hub of the platform is the source of content, origin of value, and final destination of all who travel along the spokes. It's where you want connections to ultimately arrive. It's also where you store most of your content.

From the hub, you share links and references to the spokes. For example, to attract connections and advocate your mission, you create a manifesto. This manifesto is posted, one time, at the hub. Then you share the link, a brief introduction, and an attention-grabbing graphic to all the spokes.

The spokes are where your stakeholders already gather, so it's natural for them to expect relevant content at the end of the spoke. While browsing with friends on their favorite personal social media platform, they come across a link someone shared to your hub. When they see the link to your manifesto, attracted by the graphic and introduction as well as the interest from their friend, they click the link and are taken to your hub.

Once at the hub, stakeholders read your manifesto and see other relevant content. They may now choose to take action. You may want them to apply for a job, make a donation, or spread the word about your mission to their friends. Any action or conversion you seek can be achieved at the hub.

Reach
While the hub serves the purpose of leverage to maximize your investment and content, the spokes serve to maximize your reach. The more spokes extending from your hub, the greater your reach. The point is that a spoke enables you to

extend your network to meet existing and potential stakeholders where they gather.

Extending our example above, your manifesto, posted in a discussion forum for professionals with similar interests, will draw interest from many members in that forum. This reach brings professionals from that forum back to your hub. Ideally, many of them will sign up to follow and contribute. Back at the spoke, some forum members may not even click the link, but will share it with their own network instead. This extends the reach even further, effectively turning the end of the spoke into a sub-hub. From that forum member, there are many new spokes extending out, and reach is amplified exponentially.

Global

Leverage and reach are unlimited in a technical platform. Major social networks are international—if not global—in reach, and the Internet itself knows no bounds. As technologies evolve, the role of automated translation tools increase the global nature of digital platforms. As a result, the leader is able to convert connections in any region or language.

Conversion

Of course, leverage and reach are meaningless if you can't convert. In the field of web analytics (the study of web traffic, visitors, etc.), conversion is a generic term for a sale, subscription, video view, review submittal, or whatever action you want a visitor to take.

As a leader, you could have countless objectives for your stakeholders. Whatever your objective, the completion of that objective by an individual is a conversion. Some examples:

- A non-profit CEO seeking volunteers converts with each new volunteer to sign up.

- A politician seeking signatures on a petition converts with each new signature.
- An author seeking reviews of their new book obtains a conversion with each review.

The key is that these conversions are happening through each leader's platform. These are the objectives you have as a leader. However, as a leader, your objective may not be as easily identifiable as a signature, review, or some other hard fact. This is where the double meaning of a conversion helps us.

According to Dictionary.com, conversion can also be defined as a:[24]
- change in character, form, or function.
- spiritual change from sinfulness to righteousness.
- change from one religion, political belief, viewpoint, etc., to another.
- change of attitude, emotion, or viewpoint from one of indifference, disbelief, or antagonism to one of acceptance, faith, or enthusiastic support, especially such a change in a person's religion.

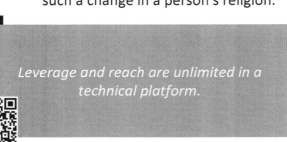

Leverage and reach are unlimited in a technical platform.

As a leader, isn't this also what you seek? Changes in character or belief, or the strengthening of one's faith are positives that a leader would want to see in her own life as well as in the lives of the people she serves. Whichever conversion you seek, your leverage, reach, and opportunities for increased conversion are enhanced through your platform and social media presence.

Increasing conversion is not the only way the social media platform benefits a leader, though. It will also be a great benefit when you get into trouble.

When You Mess Up

Rest assured, you will make mistakes. No great leader is free of mistakes. Worse, whether you directly make the mistakes or not, you will be held accountable for other people's mistakes. Remember Obama's dead grandmother? It may not have even been our company, but a contractor entrusted with keys to the account that caused the incident. That did not matter—brand leadership was accountable.

Whether you are directly responsible or not, there will be a social media crisis sometime in your career. When these crises occur, it's too late to build your platform, connections, and influence. This must be in place for months—even years— before you need it. Otherwise your connections will undervalue your presence. Worse, any attempt to build a platform following a crisis will be interpreted as too little too late.

The leader with an existing platform has several benefits during a crisis:

1. Connections
2. Influence
3. Listening Tools
4. Forum
5. Social Proof

1. Connections

Connections provide strength in numbers. The more followers, subscribers, and fans a leader has, the greater their opportunity to get the word out to a broader network. Social media crises can spread like a brush fire during a drought. Fighting that fire is easier when you have more firefighters. Similarly, in a social media crisis, the larger your network, the more connections you have to counter the escalating matter. For more on this, see the "Connect" section under "Principles."

2. Influence

Influence is about your ability to gain the support of members in the community. If you already have an existing platform, you will have greater influence than a leader who does not. Stakeholders know you. They listen to you and want to hear what you have to say. This is why they are on the platform and share your content. These stakeholders are willing ears, waiting to hear your response.

3. Listening Tools

Your platform offers you a variety of ways in which you can listen to your stakeholders. These include reading direct messages, observing their discussion in forums, and following what they like and dislike. Furthermore, you can set up specific solutions to notify you when key words or sentiment arise. We cover this more in the "Listen" section under "Principles." For now, just understand that these listening tools provide leaders the capability to quickly and clearly understand shifting sentiments in the community. In the midst of a crisis, this is enormously helpful. For example, if you want to know which stakeholders are standing up for you and your organization, listening tools give you this ability. Additionally, if you want to know who your greatest detractors are, you can find them here. Through these components of your platform, you can gauge the sentiment of the crowd and know if your actions have an impact.

4. Forum

Your forum is a place to meet and communicate directly with your audience. During a crisis, the subscribers to your content will meet you here to discuss your response to the issue. This is like the press room of the White House. At any given moment, all you need to do is ask, and members of your platform will arrive to hear you and respond. Sure, they may not be there live, but they'll quickly receive messages shared through your platform. The engagement is high because these connections have already invested in you as a leader. Your virtual forum is your sounding board.

5. Social Proof

Social proof is evidence that you are respected and appreciated by a community. This is measurable online. For example, anyone questioning the degree to which other individuals respect and value your message can easily count subscribers, positive feedback, and traffic on your platform. Consider this against a leader lacking such a platform. The leader with the platform has documented validation readily available. In contrast, the leader lacking a platform must first provide their background and experience to establish credibility. The time required establishing credibility can be very costly during a crisis.

Without a pre-existing platform, a leader facing a crisis is at a major loss as opposed to one who already has strength in connections, influence, listening tools, forums, and social proof. Wouldn't you rather have a platform in place when you need it?

You are fortunate to have the capabilities of a digital platform in your leadership tool kit. Leaders in previous generations were not as fortunate. Those leaders lacked the benefits of contemporary social media. Yet there were plenty of successful leaders in history.

To be equally effective, leaders today need to leverage the tools available to them. These include key components of their platform. Without a platform in place, you will be at a disadvantage compared with the competition. To maximize your reach, influence, and responsiveness in times of crisis, build a hub and spoke model platform.

Your Platform Summary

I introduced this section by explaining the origins of platforms. Platforms originated as anything that elevated a speaker so their message could be heard further away. These included pulpits for priests, balconies for kings, and soap boxes for rebels. Today, the platform is used for the same purpose—enabling the leader to be heard by more people. However, the digital revolution means these platforms reach further and enable greater dialogue. Advances in social media platforms enable leaders to finally lead in a more personal manner through a mass dialogue.

I then examined the three primary platform models: Stronghold, Spider Web, and Hub and Spoke models. Each model has positives and negatives, but the ideal for most leaders today is the Hub and Spoke. This model enables the maximum reach at the lowest effort and cost. Leaders with a Hub and Spoke platform create and store most of their content in a central location, such as a primary website, intranet, or page on a third-party site. This is their hub. Then, these leaders reach out to stakeholders, meeting them where they are, often on other platforms.

I also explained the many benefits of a platform for leaders. These included leverage and reach. Leverage is all about maximizing your benefits and minimizing your effort by building resources for your communications and mission in a central location. Then, one can extend the reach of that hub by connecting to others and pointing them back to the primary location. You will find all these benefits especially helpful when you or your organization gets into trouble. Having the value of a platform ready to help you get out of trouble is vital for today's leaders.

Reflection
1. What components of a platform do you have today?
2. What components of a platform do other leaders in your field or industry have?
3. How can you build or strengthen your platform?

YOUR PRINCIPLES

"The first responsibility of a leader is to define reality. The last is to say thank you. In between, the leader is a servant."

—Max de Pree

The principles of effective leadership have not changed for thousands of years. What has changed is the technology enabling leaders to practice these principles. The greatest leaders today understand the timeless core principles of leadership, but apply them in contemporary channels.

Revolution

Welcome to the social media revolution. Like many revolutions before this, winners and losers will be influenced by leadership principles. As a leader in this generation, you need to be familiar with these principles, if you want to achieve your mission.

In this section, we'll look at historic leaders from the American Revolution as models, reviewing how the two sides exercised various leadership principles. We'll analyze the successful practices of patriotic American colonists followed by an explanation of how British loyalists failed to practice the same principles.

After looking at historic examples of these principles, we'll look at contemporary successes and failures by leaders in the social media revolution. The objective is to enable you to most successfully apply these principles to your own movement.

Principle Overview

Acronyms help me comprehend and recollect key concepts. So, when I made the connection between revolutionary social media leadership principles across the ages, I worked from the most obvious acronym: S-O-C-I-A-L. That said, in social media, listening always comes first (I'll explain why below). Therefore, we'll cover these principles in reverse order. Here's an overview of the principles:

L—Listen

Listen to your stakeholders. Understanding their pains and needs is vital.

A—Action-Oriented

Of course, it's not enough to simply listen. You must also be capable of action.

I—Integrity

Integrity is paramount for leaders. Social media amplifies the necessity of this principle.

C—Connect

Leaders must connect across many social networks and value the connections of others.

O—Open

The most successful leaders in a revolution are transparent about intentions and decisions.

S—Serve

If you're not serving others, you're self-serving, and that's not leading. Stakeholders see this.

Learning from Our Mistakes

I want to take a moment for an important side note, before we look at specific individuals for examples of leadership principles. I believe we are all broken people. We all have failures and must learn from our mistakes. The individuals highlighted here are neither perfect nor inherently bad. Instead, what we review below are snapshots in time—single point examples.

If you visit my blog (ModernServantLeader.com), you will find, among my most popular posts, a series on my greatest failures and the lessons I learned from those failures. I shared those posts in the hope of saving others from the same mistakes. I am grateful to the leaders referenced here for precisely that: the opportunity to learn from them, including their failures.

Now, let's begin our review of the principles by understanding how we listen to stakeholders.

S-O-C-I-A-L Leadership Principles

Being a leader is not easy, but the tools available today make it easier than ever before. Can you imagine what great historic leaders would have done with today's technology?

> What would Abraham Lincoln do with a social network spanning the North and the South?

> Do you think the Apostles would use digital syndication to spread the good news?

> What would Martin Luther King, Jr. do with the ability to distribute sermons live, globally?

> What would Henry Ford do with terabytes of consumer preference data at his fingertips?

Leaders today must grab this opportunity to listen to stakeholders everywhere. You cannot ignore the voice of stakeholders, because the world hears them. That's a challenge and an opportunity. The opportunity starts with listening.

Listen

Industry experts agree that when it comes to social media engagement, it is important that you listen first. A failure to do so could spell disaster for leaders and their organizations. Fortunately for the colonial patriots in the American

Revolution, they knew how to listen. Let's look at how the colonial patriots demanded that England listen.

Colonial Patriots

James Otis, a Boston politician during the American Revolution, wrote, "Taxation without representation is tyranny." This phrase was later adapted to become the often-quoted rallying cry of Patriots leading up to the revolution: "No taxation, without representation!"

> *You cannot ignore the voice of stakeholders, because the world hears them.*

In fact, prior to the war, most colonists were not in favor of separation from Britain. Many did not even object to the taxes imposed by Britain. What they objected to was their lack of say in what taxes they received. Because there was no representation for them in Parliament, they felt it was unjust for decisions to be made that impacted their livelihood.

The colonial patriots listened to their neighbors. They understood the needs of fellow colonists and voiced this in publications like that of James Otis. In short, what angered colonists was Britain's lack of ability to do the same listening. Still, King George III refused to listen.

King George III

In response to the colonists' cry to be heard, King George argued that the people already had a form of virtual representation. In essence, Parliament was in place to hear the concerns of the colonists and take them into consideration. Regardless of the fact that no members of Parliament lived in the colonies or had their primary homes there, they were supposed to represent the concerns of the people there. A common complaint about leaders is their ruling from an "ivory tower," casting orders down to the masses below. These leaders do not see or experience the results of the decisions they make. The colonists perceived their British rulers in this light.

It's easy to understand why the colonists remained angered with the lack of their British leaders' willingness to listen. This anger and frustration fueled the fires leading up to the Revolution.

Much like Britain should have listened to the colonists early, before the Revolution, you should listen first, before engaging in discussions on social media channels. If you do not do so, you risk responding to the wrong questions or engaging in an unwelcome manner.

Answering the Wrong Question

Failure to listen could mean you jump into one detail of a much broader issue. For example, an auto manufacturer entering a car enthusiast forum to provide a simple solution to a faulty wiring problem may miss the bigger point. This one question may be part of a much larger concern on declining quality. While the community will be happy to see the manufacturer represented, they will also expect a response to their much larger quality concerns. A willingness to answer the very specific issue while not responding to the larger quality issue will be perceived as a dismissal of the larger issue, a lack of concern for consumers, or worse, ignorance. To ensure you do not answer the wrong question, listen first.

Unwelcome Manner

Many communities grow, in part, because they are considered exclusive. This exclusivity may be formal and intentional, or informal and implied. In either case, your participation may not be welcome in some communities. For example, a community you perceive to be about your industry in general may actually be targeted primarily at your competition. While listening in such a forum could have obvious benefits, your candid engagement is likely not desired. As a result, the fans and advocates of your competition may not welcome your participation. Call it a bit of the "pilgrims in an unholy land" syndrome.[25]

Whether you answer the wrong question or respond in an unwelcome manner, any failure to listen to stakeholders can hurt your objectives as a leader. ConAgra Food and their agency, Ketchum, learned this the hard way in the modern world of social media.

Ketchum and ConAgra Food

Unfortunately, Ketchum and ConAgra Food failed to listen before initiating a social media campaign of their own. In a marketing campaign for ConAgra's Marie Callender brand of microwaveable lasagna, Ketchum planned a special dinner for food bloggers ("foodies") and mommy bloggers. The mommy bloggers alone may have made the program a success, but not the foodies; I'll explain why below, but first, the story . . .

Foodies and mommy bloggers received a formal invitation for them and a guest to dinner at Sotto Terra, an "intimate Italian restaurant," with TLC celebrity Chef George Duran and "supermarket guru" Phil Lempert. The invitation explained the evening's plans:[26]

> *"You and a guest are invited to dine at Sotto Terra, an intimate Italian restaurant in New York City. While being served a delicious four-course meal, you will learn about the latest food trends from Phil, engage in conversation with new friends and sample George's one-of-a-kind sangria. The evening will also feature giveaways and a surprise at the end!"*

The term surprise was an understatement. Many of the foodies invited out to the dinner had very specific concerns about mass-produced food. Their concerns included issues like food coloring chemicals, high sodium content, and other relevant issues. You can imagine their surprise when these foodies were unknowingly fed exactly that.

One food blogger summarized the sentiment well, when she wrote:[27]

> *"I'm NOT their target consumer, and they were totally off by thinking I would buy or promote their highly processed frozen foods after tricking me to taste it."*

As a result, there was an outcry by offended bloggers— especially the foodies. It was clear that the publicity stunt backfired.

If you put yourself in their shoes, you can almost understand how things went wrong. After all, Pizza Hut and other companies pulled off similar stunts with great success. The difference is that Pizza Hut knew their stakeholders. Those invited to and surprised at their events were not advocates against the very product with which they were presented. That is where Ketchum and ConAgra failed. Their leaders did not understand their stakeholders. They did not listen.

In their defense, ConAgra decided to cancel the last evening. More importantly, the company never used the footage, effectively cancelling the entire campaign.

Unfortunately, the net result was a substantial investment by ConAgra and Ketchum with the only result being negative press for the brand and product that they intended to promote. A search for ConAgra Ketchum and food blogger today reveals eleven hundred pieces of content about this incident, all because the leaders failed to listen to their stakeholders first.[28]

To avoid this problem, Ketchum and ConAgra Foods should have listened to social media advocate and consultant, Chris Brogan. Chris Brogan understands the need to listen to stakeholders. He preaches the concept of listening and its importance to social media leaders everywhere.

Chris Brogan

Chris Brogan is a best-selling author, advocate, and consultant in the social media space. His books, including *Trust Agents*, *Impact Equation* (both co-authored with Julien Smith), and *Social Media 101*, are among the must-reads for anyone developing a social media strategy. At the time of this writing, Chris has over sixty-seven thousand blog subscribers and two hundred eighteen thousand social media platform followers (with a seven hundred to one follower ratio),[29] and over one hundred thousand people include him in yet another platform. When Chris speaks on social media, people listen, and Chris often speaks about listening to your stakeholders.

Chris explains the importance of creating a "listening station":

> *I'm a huge proponent of professional listening as part of a business communication strategy. Lots of people will sell you ways to speak. They'll give you lots of ways to get your message all over the place. Me? I'm passionate about listening as much as I am speaking. You know: two ears, one mouth, that stuff.* —Chris Brogan (ChrisBrogan.com)

Chris explains how to create a free listening station using common tools. By compiling search queries that will automatically inform you of new content relevant to your brand, you ensure that you're seeing much of the discussion by, or about, your stakeholders. The process is as simple as a web search, with a couple of extra steps, like providing your email address and determining the frequency of updates.

Listening Tools and Techniques

There are some great tools for listening available to leaders today. Of course, the technology is constantly evolving, so we'll focus less on the tool itself and more on the concept. There are three categories of listening: comprehensive, real-time, and analytical.

Comprehensive Listening

In order to truly listen comprehensively, I suppose a leader would have to spend their entire day doing nothing but reading and listening. Even then, I suspect much of the relevant content would be missed. That said, there are listening approaches that are more comprehensive than others. This is what comprehensive listening is about: the *most* comprehensive category of listening.

Comprehensive listening takes time, as it involves scanning multiple sites, platforms, sources, and other types of content. Therefore, you need to commission a tool that can handle such a load and provide you with regular updates.

Web Alerts

Any search engine should be able to provide you with these alerts[30]. Simply tell the search engine what keywords you are interested in, and it will let you know when new content containing those words is found.

Examples may include your brands, products, and services, or those of your competitors. You may also want to include your own name to catch direct mentions of yourself. Then just set how often you want to be notified. Based on the settings you provide, the search engine will send you updates, enabling you to listen in a comprehensive manner.

Content you may miss includes anything the search engines cannot index. These include private sites for which registration is required and other pages where the site owners ask search engines not to index the content.

If you have difficulty finding or creating this comprehensive listening solution through a search engine, there are other options. First, there are plenty of text analytics tools on the market designed for scanning the web. Furthermore, you could hire an agency to conduct this effort for your organization. Whatever solution you use, make sure you are regularly reviewing, or at least skimming, such relevant content updates.

Real-Time Listening

Real-time listening is more acute. Simply put, these are streams of relevant content updates you can monitor throughout the day. As a busy executive, you may prefer to delegate these responsibilities. However, before you dismiss this opportunity, consider how I use real-time monitoring.

Depending upon which office I am at, I keep at least two monitors open. On the left-hand screen, I typically have a real-time monitoring window open. There are many tools available for simple real-time monitoring[31]. Most often, leaders begin real-time monitoring within a social media dashboard tool. To find one for yourself, search the web for "social media dashboard tool."

Social media dashboard tools enable users to connect many social media platform accounts to a single user screen. From that screen you can read and write posts across connected platforms. As a result, these make great tools for live-streaming relevant posts across multiple platforms.

For example, the monitor on my dashboard has several streams of content displayed, such as:

1. Brands (including the brands with which I work daily)
2. Competitors (brand and company names of competitors in the industries in which I work)
3. Leadership Terms (such as "leadership," "executive," "CEO," and "Servant Leadership")
4. Social Media ("social," "Social Media," "#Social," "Social Network," "Social Technology")
5. My Connections (updates from those I follow)
6. Direct Messages and Replies (any messages sent directly to me)

Now, I certainly can't watch this monitor constantly. However, when a stream sees a lot of action, like the Brand and Competitor streams, I know something is up. This becomes apparent because a stream that normally only displays a couple of new posts an hour suddenly starts displaying new posts every minute.

If I notice a higher-than-normal activity level in a stream from the corner of my eye, I pull it up and see what's happening. I certainly don't catch every breaking issue, but it helps, and it keeps me aware and engaged throughout the day. Essentially, I am tuned in to the global dialogue, real-time, whenever I want to be. You should consider a similar solution to keep yourself engaged throughout the day.

A Real-Time Example
This is precisely how I first noticed the Obama incident that occurred in our brand. During the presidential debate, I had the real-time monitors open on my laptop, sitting on the coffee table in front of me. The stream monitoring that brand name had been quiet all night. When it suddenly sprang to life with activity, scrolling new posts every second, I knew something had happened. In fact, all I did was scroll over to the real-time monitor stream from our actual brand accounts, and it was all too clear what had happened.

Had I not had those real-time monitors open, I surely would have heard about it in the morning. In fact, I'd likely have heard it on the morning news. If not there, my comprehensive monitor would have told me. In social media time, though, that's too late for a leader to respond.

Large companies employ real-time monitoring with dedicated employees and full-scale communication monitoring rooms. For the average leader or small company, such a dedicated organization may be a luxury you cannot afford. All the same, it's good to have available and becomes even better when paired with comprehensive listening and the last form: analytical listening.

Analytical Listening

You simply cannot capture all relevant content. Even with comprehensive and real-time listening, there will be plenty that slips through. Furthermore, reading and responding to individual posts does not capture trends like overall sentiment and share of voice.

Sentiment

Thanks to social media technology, you are now able to track the sentiment of stakeholders better than ever before. There is still an art to this science, but many companies are developing advanced analytical engines to measure the sentiment of discussions occurring online. Are your consumers happy, angry, confused, or indifferent? Wouldn't you love to know? Well, with thousands of data points online to analyze, you can now get a pretty good idea.

Analytical listening tools scan thousands, if not millions, of posts mentioning your keywords. They then analyze each post for terms reflecting the sentiments of the poster. Are there a lot of curse words? Then it's likely a sentiment of anger. Perhaps there are several question marks. This denotes confusion. Of course, this is an overly simplified example.

Nonetheless, when you combine the analysis of millions of data points, the sentiment analysis becomes almost frighteningly accurate. Like any form of automated technology gauging human reaction, there will be errors. However, across the full spectrum of content analyzed, your results should be directionally accurate.

Share of Voice

Who are stakeholders more interested in—you or the competition? The old-world factor in business (which is still relevant, of course) is market share: the percentage of overall market that a company or product controls. This measurement was usually computed as the percentage of total stock value within the industry that company or product held.

The new-world—and increasingly relevant—metric is share of voice. By analyzing thousands of discussions and posts, you can assess who is the topic of discussion. A similar analysis can be done by computing the total number of mentions across an industry online. Whatever portion of that total includes mentions of your organization or product is your share of voice.

Combining the share of voice metric with the sentiment analysis, you have a pretty good forecast of where market share is heading. For example, if your competitor has eighty percent of the share of voice and the sentiment of that content is seventy percent negative, you're well positioned to take market share away. But wait—the twenty percent share of voice your brands hold has a sentiment largely of confusion. Therefore, you'll need to dig into what your customers are confused about before you can pull that market share away from the competition.

In order to understand what is really happening online at the macro level, you need analytical tools. You can't measure an ocean with a teaspoon. These tools will measure the sentiment of stakeholders, as well as the share of voice you hold. Of course, other numbers, like sheer number of posts and other content, are also helpful, in addition to the old-school (circa 1999) traffic metrics. If all of these numbers scare you, you may want to enlist the assistance of a data analyst.

Listen Recap

So we see how James Otis ignited the patriotic colonists by highlighting the lack of listening from their tyrannical leaders in Britain. In response, King George III and Parliament continued to turn a deaf ear to America. To prevent such failures today, Chris Brogan explains the importance of listening in social media by creating a listening station. This is a principle Ketchum and ConAgra Foods failed to practice, resulting in a disastrous publicity stunt. To be an effective leader in the social media revolution, you must listen to your stakeholders. You do this by enlisting the right technology and processes for comprehensive, real-time, and analytical listening.

> *You can't measure an ocean with a teaspoon.*

Of course, you can't just listen all the time. In fact, we know that speed matters in social media. Therefore, you must also have a propensity for action.

Action-Oriented

A recent study found that the half-life of social media posts is about three hours.[32] This means that fifty percent of people who read your social content see it within the first three hours. Waiting to see what happens is not a strategy; it's avoidance. As a result, you and your team need to be ready to take action at all times.

The need to be action-oriented in leadership is nothing new. History is full of leaders who seized the moment when it was ripe for picking or, in contrast, let opportunity rot on the vine. Paul Revere and the patriots understood this principle.

One if by Land, Two if by Sea

What American is not familiar with the phrase "One if by land, two if by sea"? On the night before the American Revolution broke out, patriots awaited the first move by the British military. They expected the British to march on Lexington and Concord (Massachusetts), where the patriots stored munitions. The arrest of patriot leaders Samuel Adams and John Hancock along the way was also a distinct possibility.

In order to prepare for this advance, the plan was set: if the British were about to move south, over the land route to Lexington and Concord, a single lantern would hang in the old North Chapel. If, instead, the expectation was that the British would move north, over the sea route, then two lanterns would hang from the chapel.

This warning sign would alert backup riders across the river, in case the primary riders (including Paul Revere) were arrested. This way, backup riders could head to Lexington and Concord, alerting patriots, especially Samuel Adams and John Hancock.

As patriots in Boston noticed British troops preparing the ships and overheard the military planning something big the next morning, the news reached Paul Revere. It seemed that the British planned to move across the sea, on the northern route. The order was given, and two lanterns were hung from atop the old North Church.

Risk identified. Decision made. Action taken.

Notice the simplicity and effectiveness of this message. Colonial patriots did not write a thirty-page memo explaining the basis for their decision. The team did not spell out all the risks, alternatives, and liabilities. There was no disclaimer that recipients of the message had to acknowledge. No privacy policy. No terms of use. The patriots identified the risk, made a critical decision, and took action.

> *Waiting to see what happens is not a strategy. It's avoidance.*

Lord Cornwallis (British Commander)

Contrast the patriots' propensity for action with Lord Cornwallis' hesitancy early in the war. Lord Cornwallis had trapped Washington and his troops against the Hudson River near New York. With one strike, he had the chance to destroy much of the Colonial army and end the war. However, he had a tough decision to make.

Cornwallis' men had been marching all day. They were tired and weary from earlier battle. Cornwallis was faced with a decision: he could attack now and likely win the day, or he could delay the attack until morning, when his troops would be fresher and most likely sustain fewer casualties. Cornwallis received conflicting recommendations from his generals. Some felt he must attack immediately, while others urged patience. In the end, it was reported that Cornwallis said:

> *We have run down the old fox, and we will bag him in the morning.*

While this quote has been challenged, the decision not to attack remained. The result was a missed opportunity for the British.

Washington took action that evening, leaving a small contingent behind to tend fires and maintain the appearance that his army remained. Then, under cover of fog, his army escaped over the river. In the morning, Cornwallis and the British troops rode in for battle, only to find an empty camp. Their lack of action cost them dearly.

Leaders who understand the critical value of being action-oriented are still successful today. In Newark, New Jersey, not far from where Cornwallis' inaction failed him, Mayor Cory Booker took action to lead successfully hundreds of years later.

Cory Booker

It's the winter of 2010, and a massive blizzard is rolling into the east coast. Many cities are unprepared. One mayor even leaves for vacation in Florida. Sure enough, the storm hits, and it is a whopper. Social platforms are aglow with people blasting mayors and city leadership in general, wherever there is trouble.

Cory Booker sees the trouble in his great city and grabs two items: his smartphone and his shovel. Then, he hits the city streets. As he goes out to be among his stakeholders, he sees concerns being raised on social media like this one from Linda H.:

> **Linda H. (@MsXmasBaby):** @CoryBooker Is there any city volunteers to dig someone out? I am going to have Medical procedure done.

To which Cory Booker responds:

> **Cory Booker (@CoryBooker):** I just dug out your car. All the best.

That's right. The mayor personally dug out her car. Now how's that for serving your constituents? And that's not all. It's not like he walked over to one person's house because it happened to be convenient. No, the social scene is full of examples of Booker's action-oriented measures that day. There is even a video clip of the mayor pushing out a car, in which the person recording says, "We were just talking about him . . . maybe he's not so bad after all . . . "[33] Throughout the day, this mayor directed plows to streets as his stakeholders cried for help. When he could, he showed up himself, shovel in hand.

A search for content about Booker's effort that snowy day turns up over one hundred forty thousand results.[34] Perhaps though, the greatest benefits of his hard work were the personal connections he made that day; the one-on-one interactions he shared with stakeholders and the opinions he changed for the better—all were made possible through an action-oriented approach.

Storms will come and go. It is how leaders handle the storm that matters. Unlike Booker, Kenneth Cole should have better handled a storm that he created.

Kenneth Cole

Kenneth Cole, the fashion designer, has a long string of success to his name. Perhaps more importantly, he's well recognized as a philanthropist with great concern for social justice. Unfortunately, this passion did not stop him from posting a very insensitive comment as the Arab Spring was breaking out in Cairo, Egypt:

> **Kenneth Cole (@KennethCole):** Millions are in uproar in #Cairo. Rumor is they heard our new spring collection is now available online at http://bit.ly/KCairo -KC

The insensitivity of this post was clear to the majority of his connections. However, Cole's other failure, from which we can learn the most, was his lack of timeliness in responding to the backlash his post created. A comprehensive response from Cole took several hours. Yes, that's right, I said several *hours*. In traditional media, a response within the same day may be considered very quick. In social media, hours can influence an eternity of results. Consider what happened in the several hours it took Kenneth Cole to construct a solid response.

Storms will come and go. It is how leaders handle the storm that matters.

Mock Accounts

Within minutes[35] of the original post, the @KennethColePR account is created; shortly thereafter, @FakeKennethCole account is also created. Both accounts quickly gain thousands of followers as they mock Kenneth Cole's insensitive promotion attempts. Posts from these accounts suggest insensitive marketing from the man and the brand. Examples of posts from these Kenneth Cole mock accounts include:[36]

- Rolling through Germany? Gestapo by our new Berlin store!
- Searching for your missing daughter in Aruba? At least, you don't need to be a van der SLEUTH to find her resort wear!
- Ready to hang yourself 'cuz of dad's ponzi schemes? You won't be able to resist our croc-skin belts.
- George Bush doesn't care about black people. But we care about people wearing black!
- When our casual menswear line goes on sale, our outlet store is gonna be a Fort Hoodie Massacre.[37]

Social Following

With the assistance of the mock accounts, a new hashtag is launched, making it easy for others to follow the discussion, anger, and humor. As a result, #KennethColetweets begins trending high on the platform, raising awareness and attention among the social media community.

Main Stream Media Following

Soon after, the conversation leaps from social media circles to mainstream media. Before the day is up, news outlets including *The Huffington Post*, CNBC, Tech Crunch, and *NY Daily News* all have articles on the designer's faux pas.

Today, there are approximately three hundred twenty-nine thousand posts on the incident.[38] Included among the content is Kenneth Cole's good, sincere apology. His sincerity and heartfelt regret is actually a great example of how to address a mistake in social platforms—it just took much too long to get out.

Furthermore, the account has been reworked to clearly be Kenneth Cole's personal account and no longer part of the official brand communication efforts. In fact, the updated bio for @KennethCole reflects some of the lessons learned from this incident:

@KennethCole
Designer, Aspiring Humanitarian, Frustrated Activist, Social Networker In training. My tweets are not representative of the corporate @kennethcoleprd feed.

In social media, hours can influence an eternity of results.

The lesson here is not, "never make a mistake." However, action-orientation is vital for successful leaders in social media. If you have the powerful resources of a major brand, you need to have effective monitoring (see the "Listen" section above), keeping an eye out for trending disasters. Without such resources, you need to be sensitive to potential issues.

If you're sending a sensitive post, consider how others may interpret it. If there is a high risk of offending others, ensure that you can actively monitor the response for a while after posting. Sending a sensitive post just before going into a movie theatre, where you'll be offline for several hours, is a bad idea. It's best to send such a post when you know you will be actively monitoring the situation from your desk all day.

Action-Oriented Tools and Techniques

Being an action-oriented leader is all about being prepared (the scout masters of my youth would be proud). Being prepared means being ready to respond to a variety of different situations. These situations include maximizing good opportunities as well as minimizing damage from negative incidents. Below are some examples.

Speed

I've gotten a lot of pushback on the expectation of responses within hours. Specifically, my reflection that Kenneth Cole should have responded much more quickly and that other leaders should be expected to do the same. I understand these concerns. Responding within hours can be tough. But it's not as tough as many think.

The important message around speed in social media is to be responsive. Reasonable stakeholders don't expect comprehensive responses in minutes. However, they do expect acknowledgement within hours. In other words, Kenneth Cole was not required to give a comprehensive apology in minutes. Still, he should have immediately recognized his faux pas and retracted it in less time. In the same manner, a leader who sees positive sentiment suddenly skyrocket online needs to immediately engage in the conversation. You don't have to provide tons of new content or legal-approved messaging, but you do have to be present *during* the conversation. In social media it is truly fifteen minutes of fame, not hours. Leaders can't maximize those fifteen minutes if it takes them six hours to respond.

Those who struggle with the magnitude of responsiveness that social media demands need to adapt. It's uncomfortable, I understand. However, this is the world we live in. When responding in social media, think in minutes instead of hours and hours instead of days. If your first response in social media is days out, you will be too late.

> *In social media it is truly fifteen minutes of fame, not hours.*

Template Messages

In order to prepare for a variety of scenarios, you should draft template messages. For example, if a celebrity suddenly promotes your work, do you have a discount or promotion available that celebrity could share with their fans? You also want to have a message ready in case something you posted was misinterpreted or received badly, like Kenneth Cole's #Cairo hijack. If he had had a heartfelt, sincere message template, he could have quickly tailored and posted it before so many major news outlets covered the story.

Now, it is very important that you remain *authentic* in your message. Once you draft template messages, it will become all too easy to respond without being genuinely interested and displaying that interest to recipients. The point is not to be disingenuous, but to have the bulk of a message ready, so you can tailor it as appropriate and still be quick to respond.

Templates enable you to focus your energy on the higher-value task of understanding the individual(s) to whom you respond, rather than worrying about the less-intuitive introduction, closing, or signature statements. For example, when sending a response to new connections, there are usually two tasks I complete to tailor the message and reflect my sincere interest:

1. Names
Dale Carnegie once reminded us "a person's name is to that person the sweetest and most important sound in any language." For this reason and more, I use the person's name. In fact, I usually use the name twice: once in the standard introduction and again before closing.

2. Website/Profile
If the contact lists a website in their signature or profile, I visit and at least skim it to provide some quick feedback. This feedback may be as simple as "I really liked your site," or, if the content is particularly relevant, I may point to specific posts or quotes that I enjoyed. If they don't list a website, I often comment on their profile/biography information. These comments range from "Go <insert professional sports team name of their city/state>!" (assuming I like their team) to commenting on a cool quote from their biography information.

Remember, templates are not just for handling the negative scenario. Consider the positive opportunities as well. These may include someone simply quoting you in a positive manner, providing great feedback on a product or service you offer, or showing interest in one of your products. Your templates should cover these scenarios as well.

Depending upon the medium or platform, there are a variety of technologies available for creating, storing, and quickly retrieving template messages. For instance, most email programs offer a template feature. As for other platforms, you may have to use a third-party provider, but the options exist. In the worst-case scenario, you can create a simple text document or a spreadsheet with quickly available copy-and-paste options.

Training

For your team, you need to conduct appropriate training. Never assume they know how to respond; ensure it by equipping them with the right tools and providing the confidence that is only available through practice. There are many aspects of training for proper action in social media—too many to cover them all here. However, some highlights include:

Boundaries

What are the boundaries of your team in social media? Are there expenses they can assume in specific situations? For example, employees of Ritz-Carlton are empowered to spend up to two thousand dollars to satisfy a guest. You may not have the margins of Ritz-Carlton, but you should have your own limits clearly defined at each level. Are there standard coupons or discount codes everyone may offer?

Escalation Points

When a problem arises that is beyond a team member's skill or authorization level, they are expected to escalate the matter to a supervisor. These guidelines are escalation points. The leader's objective should be to equip, enable, and empower stakeholder communication at all levels, so keep the escalation expectations to a minimum. An example of this is the entire communication policy for Zappos.com employees. It reads:[39]

Be real and use good judgment.

That said, the team needs to know when it is clearly expected that they escalate an issue, if for no other reason than to raise awareness. Remember to consider escalation points for positive messages as well. Some sample scenarios for escalation in social media may include:

- **Number of Followers**: If a user complains or praises you, does the number of people following that individual influence how you respond?
- **Follower Ratio**: A more accurate determinant of influence, the follower ratio of an individual (following/followers), may tell your team when they should escalate a matter.
- **Frequency of Posts**: Does the number of times an individual complains about or praises your efforts influence your response?
- **Forum Readership**: Does the number of subscribers to the forum where a message is posted change the anticipated response?
- **Legal Matters**: Does a legal concern, such as patent infringement or customer privacy, require a different form of escalation?
- **Safety**: Most organizations agree that any time a stakeholder's physical safety is at risk, an escalation is expected.

Templates
Ensure that the team has access to and understands how to use available template responses.

Simulations
The best way to prepare your team is through simulation. Role-playing scenarios can help your team understand the perspective of all parties involved. You may want to have each team member role play their own position, that of a

complaining individual, and that of their superior, to whom a matter may be escalated. Again, remember to include the positive scenarios as well—you want your team equally prepared for the good and the bad.

The Super Example of Action-Orientation

For a great example of both templates and training, look no further than the big game itself. The professional football league's championship game monitoring station is set up for effective listening across many channels. Employees monitoring at the station are then equipped with standard responses and trained on how to respond to a variety of situations.

Traffic jam mentioned at the corner of Quarterback Way and Linebacker Drive? Suggest this alternate route. On a more serious note, has someone lost a child? Contact the police at this number.

By combining a list of ready responses with effective training, America's professional football league is ready to be action-oriented each year during the big game.

Action-Orientation Recap

A tendency toward action is an important principle for leaders. Colonial patriots knew this when they hung the lanterns in the old North Church and were grateful when Lord Cornwallis failed to use the same principle, enabling George Washington and his army to escape. Centuries later, Kenneth Cole was not so lucky. Cole's failure to respond promptly and decisively is a good lesson for any social leader. However, the best example here is clearly Cory Booker. Whether it is a winter blizzard or a storm of another form, take a page from Booker: grab your social media and your tools of the trade. Then take action.

Listening to your stakeholders is critical. Responding with quick action helps as well. However, neither of these principles will matter if the leader is not a person of integrity.

Integrity

Integrity is the moral authority one holds with their stakeholders. A leader with great integrity has strong moral authority and influence. This moral authority comes from a consistency of actions and words across personal and professional lives. Leaders with great integrity can be trusted to consistently say and act in a manner agreeable to those whom they represent. For most leaders, this includes legal, ethical, and moral behaviors in both personal and professional matters. Leaders who say one thing and do another lack integrity.

A leader lacking integrity will not hold the commitment of the people. One can, of course, control others through power, as long as they hold that power. However, with power alone, a leader will not get the best from the people. With integrity, power is not needed, and the best commitment and performance of the people can be achieved. In the American Revolution, one did not have to look far to find integrity practiced among the colonial patriots.

Patrick Henry
"Give me liberty or give me death!"

Patrick Henry pronounced his integrity with this statement in an address to the Virginia Convention. The man stood up, in front of his peers and the colonial patriots, and proclaimed that he was committed to the cause with his life. The consistency of his beliefs and actions extended to his death. No man in the room could question his integrity with respect to the pursuit of liberty.

Henry's rising speech was credited as the influence necessary to deliver Virginia troops to the revolutionary cause. Attendance at the convention included other great patriots of integrity, George Washington and Thomas Jefferson.

Estimates of the number of Virginians fighting in the war vary, but most suggest it neared one thousand men[40]—a substantial contribution to the overall war. Many of these men died in the battle and slaughter of Waxhaw, which Banastre Tarleton led.

Banastre Tarleton (British General)

Unfortunately, the British did not consistently reflect the same sense of integrity. Most men were men of honor, but they also used brutal men, like Banastre Tarleton, to get their dirty work done. If you've seen the Mel Gibson movie "The Patriot,"[41] antagonist Colonel William Tavington (played by Jason Isaacs) is loosely based on Tarleton.

According to American accounts, at the battle of Waxhaw, American troops, including many Virginians, were overrun by Tarleton's cavalry. The Americans' request for surrender was ignored, and dozens of men were slaughtered.

A leader lacking integrity will not hold the commitment of the people.

Naturally, there is dispute on the accuracy of this account. However, Tarleton argued that anyone who sympathized with revolutionaries were traitors and should therefore be punished by death. His perspective was unyielding in nature. "Bloody Ban, the Butcher," as he was eventually known, became a rallying cry for colonial troops.

The lack of integrity reflected by Tarleton inspired his adversaries, the colonial patriots. This effectively added fuel to the fire. Tarleton's lack of integrity provided examples for patriots. Angry men and women could point to Tarleton as an example of why the British could not be trusted.

Furthermore, Tarleton's men, at least those of integrity, were not inspired to support his actions or give him their best effort. After all, the British military still held honor and moral values in high regard. Tarleton's actions were, at best, questionable in this regard, thereby reflecting a lack of integrity.

Fast-forward over two hundred years, and we see how contemporary leaders of integrity serve their stakeholders. Our first example is one I mentioned earlier: Michael Hyatt.

Michael Hyatt

I included Michael Hyatt earlier, under personal leadership examples. You may recall that Michael led Thomas Nelson, the largest Christian publisher, for seven years. In that role, Hyatt represented the organization's beliefs and ideals wonderfully.

Although his social media activity clearly displayed his own opinion, Hyatt was an excellent reflection of the people and culture of Thomas Nelson. It is the responsibility of a leader to accurately reflect the people and culture to which they are accountable.

On his personal blog (MichaelHyatt.com), Hyatt's posts are both professional and personal. Most of his family members are also active on social media. They even had an account for their dog at one point. As a result, it is easy to see how Hyatt's personal life aligns with the integrity that he reflects in business.

Individuals of strong integrity, closely aligned with the integrity of their brand and organizations, provide an awesome benefit in this way. Whether the individual is speaking on a personal or professional topic, the morals, ethics, message, and behavior are consistent. This contrasts directly with many social media blunders by individuals managing social media accounts who lack the same integrity desired by the brands they represent.

We began this book by reflecting on a failure of integrity between the individual managing a social media account and the messaging of that brand. The person managing the brand account held a strong objection to President Obama and felt it appropriate to suggest to the world that Obama's grandma died because she didn't want to see him as president. Consequently, the beliefs reflected by the person managing the account were a massive contradiction to those of the brand. Had the person managing the brand account held the same integrity as the brand itself, this incident would not have occurred.

The point is that integrity matters. Simply paying a third party to manage your social media for you is a bad idea. Chrysler learned this lesson when a contractor managing their account accidentally posted, "I find it ironic that Detroit is known as the #MotorCity and yet no one here knows how to F**king drive." We saw a similar lesson with the Obama post. Simply outsourcing your social media management is a bad idea. Your vendor may not have the same integrity you expect for the brand. Instead, leaders need to practice the integrity the community expects of the organization and reflect this through their platform.

Michael Hyatt's integrity aligned with Thomas Nelson's. Hyatt's posts on Christian living, leadership, technology, and personal development attract those with similar faith and values.

Some examples of the content Michael shared on his personal blog during his role as CEO at Thomas Nelson included:[42]

- Four Temptations Christian Leaders Face
- How Christian Leaders Can Get Started with Social Media
- Advice to First-Time Authors
- How to Monetize Your Blog Without Selling Your Soul

Hyatt's integrity shines through all he does, and his business benefits as a result. Both his personal blog and his position at Thomas Nelson Publishers reflected consistent integrity. Unfortunately, the same cannot be said for former Whole Foods CEO John Mackey.

John Mackey

Imagine you're an investor trying to decide where to place your money. Doing your research, you find a person named "rahodeb" constantly praising Whole Foods—especially its CEO, John Mackey. You like the natural foods market and think it's a good place to invest. Rahodeb recommends Whole Foods and also regularly points out problems with Whole Foods' competitors. So you invest in Whole Foods.

> *It is the responsibility of a leader to accurately reflect the people and culture to which they are accountable.*

Sometime later, while Whole Foods seeks to acquire a competitor, the news breaks: "Rahodeb" *is* Whole Foods CEO, John Mackey. The name "Rahodeb" is later identified as an anagram of "Deborah," the name of Mackey's wife. It's no longer surprising that Rahodeb is such a fan of Whole Foods and Mr. Mackey.

How do you feel about the company, its leadership, and the integrity they present when the leader masks his identity like this? I wouldn't feel so great. In fact, I'd be concerned about what other secrets are being kept.

Now, integrity is the principle that comes closest to being one you either have or you don't. You hire and fire for matters of integrity; you don't train for it. It's difficult, if not impossible, to train someone to practice integrity. Still, there are a few things you should do.

Integrity Tools and Techniques

Okay, I admit it, there's really no tool available when it comes to integrity. This section is all about techniques, or perhaps better words are "methods" or "approaches."

Recruit for Values

Integrity has much to do with the personal values and ethics of an individual. Therefore, hiring and recruiting practices are critical for the organization.

Whether you are hiring for paid positions or recruiting volunteers for your team, the message is the same. Even volunteers should align with your values. A lack of alignment to the integrity and values of your organization can hurt your movement a great deal, regardless of whether the individual is paid or not.

These recruiting practices must include thorough online research, not just of the usual profiles, but of all major social media channels. Of course, this doesn't mean personal comments should be taken out of context, but it does mean that bad reputations online matter. When recruiting people, seek someone who:

- Embodies your values
- Is responsive, but willing to listen
- Practices the principles in this book

Don't forget, you are social media leaders—and really, all employees in today's world are constantly representing your organization in communications. Today's communications can spread at the speed of social networks and last forever. As a result, recruiting decisions are more critical than ever before.

Know Your Own Values

Maybe you're a one-man-band for the moment. Maybe you're not hiring or recruiting at all. How do you help ensure the practice of integrity and avoid personal failures like Mr. Mackey? The answer is similar to that of a leader who is hiring: define your own values.

By define, I don't mean "think about them." I mean truly define them. Grab a sheet of paper, and sit down in a quiet space with at least several hours free. Then get to work.

Think through many scenarios and how you expect yourself to respond. Don't cover just the obvious situations, but the grey areas as well. Here are some scenarios to consider how you would respond:

1. **Gossip**: A co-worker comes to you with a juicy piece of news about the person in the next cubicle. How do you respond?
2. **Accounting Changes**: You're asked to change capital to expense and don't believe the logic aligns with Generally Accepted Accounting Principles (GAAP).[43] Do you challenge the practice?
3. **Superior Guidance**: Your boss asks you to do something which you believe is morally wrong. Do you push back?
4. **Mask an Issue**: You're asked to hide an escalating issue on your project. Do you maintain appearances or share the risk?

5. **Job Security**: An issue is raised that conflicts with your moral compass, but you fear implications to your job. Do you follow your moral compass or the paycheck?

As a leader, there will be many times when you must decide whether to stay true to yourself or cave to others. There may even be trade-offs where a decision seems to negatively impact stakeholders, but is the right decision for your integrity.

Stay true to yourself. Do what is right, and maintain your integrity. A lack of integrity damages the influence of leaders and their movement. Malcolm X was right when he said, "If you don't stand for something, you will fall for anything."

Integrity Recap

It was the colonial patriotic leaders like Patrick Henry who set the example of integrity against the backdrop of British failures like Banastre Tarleton. Leaders today, like Michael Hyatt, set the same tone, example, and expectation for exceptional leaders. Meanwhile, we can learn from failures of integrity like that displayed by "Rahodeb," John Mackey's secret identity on the Yahoo! Finance discussion boards.

Individuals who pretend to be something they are not are frequently caught in a trap of trying to remember who they are to each person. This is not a problem for leaders with integrity. Furthermore, integrity has another benefit beyond remaining true to yourself and ensuring consistency for your stakeholders: it supports the growth of your network.

In social media, the number of people who see what you do every day can be massive. For the most connected, it is literally millions. Integrity ensures that you can connect with the masses and maintain a consistent message.

Connect

For today's most effective leaders, connecting is about embracing and expanding your influence. We can all change our own little corner of the world with the right passion, tools, and motivation. However, to really change the world—or any region larger than our immediate vicinity—we must connect. While today's technology makes it easier than ever to connect on a global scale, our forefathers in the American Revolution did a great job with what they had.

Paul Revere

You just read about Paul Revere, and you likely already knew who he was. However, have you ever heard of William Dawes?

Poor William. You know, he risked his life that same fateful night as Paul Revere's famous ride. In fact, there were dozens, if not hundreds, of men (and women) who helped spread the news that "the British are coming" that night. Yet we don't seem to know any of their names. Why is that?

In his book, *The Tipping Point*,[44] Malcolm Gladwell offers an explanation: Paul Revere was a connector. William Dawes was not.

According to Gladwell, connectors are individuals who make it a habit of meeting people in different social circles and introducing people across these circles.

Chris Brogan and Julien Smith, in their book *Trust Agents*,[45] call this being "the elbow" of every deal. As they explain it, you should try to be the elbow (or connector) as often as possible, to add great value. This value comes in the form of being someone others look to for connections, information and insight.

Because Revere was great at this, his reach into a greater array of individuals was stronger than Dawes. So Revere's message spread further, faster. For example, Revere made a stop at two houses in one town. One house belonged to a high society member, whose network was comprised of the wealthy in the town. The second house belonged to a working-class individual, whose network contained more middle-class folks. As each of those individuals ran to warn others, the news went out to two entirely different groups of people, reaching more individuals overall.

In contrast to Revere, Dawes' network was more homogeneous. When Dawes stopped at two homes, both households were in the same network of people. The individuals in those households reached the same group of people. The net result was that Dawes' communication reached a far narrower audience.

It did not matter how much each man risked. It mattered who they knew and how many different social circles those connections shared.

Of course, the objective that evening was not to be remembered. Instead, it was to get the word out as fast as possible to as many people as possible. Thanks to Paul Revere's ability to connect, this was also a success. The British met a decent resistance on their way to Lexington and Concord. Perhaps more importantly, as word continued to spread, more men came to harass the British military. As a result, the British march back to Boston was particularly painful.

Your cause may not be to prepare the troops for an invading army, but your method is the same. Leaders need to spread their message beyond an immediate group. Paul Revere's ability to connect with so many different social groups by gaining their trust and support delivered results. Make strong, quality connections across a diverse group and you won't have to fight for every inch of ground. William Dawes lacked this ability. Thus, his leadership results suffered.

Loyalist Dependency (British)

Contrast Revere's connectivity with that of the British. British forces in America constantly had to turn to those colonists still loyal to the British crown. They were dependent on these "loyalists" for information, resources, and other forms of support. However, the number of people loyal to the British crown dwindled as the war dragged on. The remaining loyalists became ever more important and required even greater support because of this.

In order to preserve their network of loyalists, British forces continuously invested more and more to sustain their base. For example, when abandoning a post, the British often had to take loyalists with them. This required an investment of men, time, and money to transport, feed, and support loyalists on their march.

Correspondingly, while the colonial network of connections grew, the British connection base shrank. The more the British support network shrank, the more money was required to sustain the network. This contrast of connections can be seen in contemporary business as well.

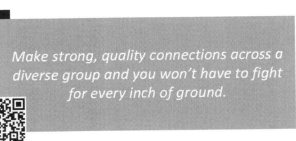

Make strong, quality connections across a diverse group and you won't have to fight for every inch of ground.

A corporation with a broad base of advocates functions like colonial patriots. These great organizations draw strength from their connections. Look at companies like Apple and

Zappos.com, who have such passionate customers they practically don't require marketing. In contrast, corporations lacking quality or a substantial base of consumer advocates must continuously invest to maintain that base. These investments come in the forms of lower price points, discounts, and higher advertising costs. Without these fiscal benefits, consumers of the latter organization are easily converted to the former.

As a leader, you want to have a strong base of loyal connections. Otherwise, the costs to sustain your base will be much higher. While Apple and Zappos.com present strong brand examples, an exemplary individual leader is Barack Obama.

Barack Obama

In case you hadn't heard, President Obama is a pretty popular guy in social media:

- Twenty-eight million fans on one platform
- Thirty-two million followers on another

As a matter of fact, in his first presidential election, Obama's campaign raised five hundred million dollars from three million online donors. Ninety-two percent of those donations were from increments of one hundred dollars or less. [46] Regardless of your political affiliations, you cannot deny that Obama changed the game by connecting better on social media than any candidate before him. Of course, the result is clear as well. Both of Obama's presidential campaigns succeeded, winning him the White House in 2008 and 2012. Obama and his campaign staff are master connectors.

Among Obama's greatest connections was the one he made with Chris Hughes, one of the founders of Facebook, to help drive Obama's social campaigns. [47] Hughes' experience designing the Facebook functionality, like the basic sharing capabilities that people love, was instrumental in building MyBarackObama.com. This digital platform for Obama's campaign contributed the critical coordination needed to build support for Obama in many key victories. One account of Hughes' contribution to the Obama campaign's social media effort says that he "helped develop the most robust set of web-based social-networking tools ever used in a political campaign, enabling energized citizens to turn themselves into activists."[48] While there are many aspects to a successful political campaign, Obama's ability to connect with such a powerful social media advocate paid off handsomely in the 2008 campaign.

Connecting may seem simple for the President of the United States, but consider this: Obama was the first U.S. President to have his own smartphone.[49] In the past, the security threat seemed too great to permit the President such a fundamental technology. Convincing the powers-that-be to permit him to carry a smartphone was challenging—even though he was the President.

Once elected, the connecting continued. Forget waiting for an official State of the Union address: when Obama wants a video out, he uses social media. Following the election, president-elect Obama began producing videos, posts, and other content about the expectations that Americans could have once he was in office. There was no waiting, and there was no change in his policy toward connecting. Direct interaction with constituents drove his success in the office and remains a key component of his leadership to date.

As other politicians learn to respect the power of connections, some organizations still fail to recognize this power. Even companies that specialize in Public Relations and media falter in this area. BrandLink Communications is one such company.

BrandLink Communication and The Bloggess

The Public Relations (PR) firm for one of the Kardashian sisters,[50] BrandLink Communications, sent out a mass pitch to mommy bloggers. Included in the distribution was a particularly influential blogger, Jenny Lawson, known as the "The Bloggess."

A standard mass-production form letter sent to The Bloggess suggested she write about a piece of fashion the Kardashianette was recently seen wearing. Now, BrandLink also failed to listen to their stakeholders (see the "Ketchum and ConAgra Food" example above) and did not realize The Bloggess' opposition to these messages. It was against Ms. Lawson's integrity to promote such nonsense just because she was asked to through a cold-copy, mass message.

All too familiar with these sorts of requests, The Bloggess had a standard message of her own. Specifically, she sent a simple note back, with a link to an image of "Wil Wheaton collating papers." This, she felt, was a balanced response to the waste of time she just received.

The page from TheBloggess.com explained her lack of interest in their request and a general offense at the time-wasting message. This, in turn, offended the PR firm.

Lawson received a note back from the original sender explaining her offense at the note, but it was essentially harmless. The Bloggess expected the issue was over. In fact, had the PR firm stopped here, there would have been no major foul. Unfortunately, they did not stop . . .

When the original sender of the message passed along Ms. Lawson's note to a Vice President of the firm, known only as "Jose," he hit the reply-all button (whether it was a mistake or not is unclear) and wrote:

> "What a f*cking b*tch!"[51]

That escalated the matter a bit. The Bloggess responded abruptly, but still in a somewhat professional tone. Her remarks were mostly focused on the failures of the PR firm to respond properly—especially given their line of work.

Jose then responded to Ms. Lawson with what could best be described as a half-hearted apology. I say half-hearted, mostly because his "apology" included the following:

> You should be flattered that you are even viewed
> relevant enough to be pitched at all.

That was the definition of the "last straw" for The Bloggess. Ms. Lawson then posted about the incident and shared it with her audience—all one hundred sixty-four thousand of them. Her subscribers responded in kind with messages of shock, dismay, and frustration of their own.

As of this writing, if you search for "BrandLink Communications," three of the top seven (first page) results are about this incident. [52] BrandLink questioned a single blogger's relevance, and she showed them how connected she was.

The beauty of it all is that Ms. Lawson likely grew her connections through this incident. Not because that was her intention, but because she reflected the key principles that social media followers seek in leaders: the principles covered here. The Bloggess concluded her post on this issue in part by stating:

> P.S. The reason I post this is not to have everyone go all
> angry-villager on the company. It's to remind other
> bloggers that there are some amazing and wonderful
> PR companies out there who will do their research and
> will make your life wonderful. And there are other PR
> companies that will try to shame you into posting their
> irrelevant spam and threaten you with talk of not using

you in the future for when they're doing advertising. Those PR firms are *ssholes, and you should probably question everything they say.

You are amazing. You are relevant. Your work is worth protecting and standing up for. And you will find wonderful PR companies to work with over time.

Those who disrespect another's connections will test the strength of their own. Jenny Lawson respects and appreciates her connections. Unfortunately for BrandLink Communications, their Vice President did not.

> *Those who disrespect another's connections will test the strength of their own.*

Connecting Tools and Techniques

At the time of this writing, one platform provides a tool[53] for visualizing connections on their platform. Below is the map of mine. In the graphic, my connections are grouped by each branch in the web. The largest group, on the left, is made up of connections primarily within or surrounding my employer for the last four years. The next largest group is related to Air Products and Chemicals Inc., where I began my career. After that is Teach For America, then Alpha Kappa Psi alumni (my college fraternity), and so on.

While this tool is a great visualization, it serves more as a reminder and conceptual framing than anything else. The idea is not that you should be specifically comparing your network map to another person, but to keep this in mind when communicating with others. This is especially true when recruiting people for your team.

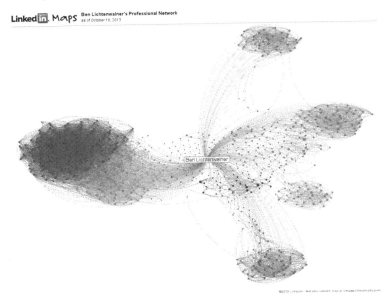

Figure 4: LinkedIn Labs map of my network

Neither broad networks nor narrow ones are good or bad. Instead, it depends upon your objectives. In most cases, a broad network, such as Paul Revere had, will gain the greatest leverage through a broader reach. However, if you seek to influence a great number of people in one organization or area, a narrow network may be best.

If you seek to go deeper into a particular network or group of individuals, you want several people with strong connections in that area. Their network map would largely cover that area and overlap a great deal with yours or other individuals already in the organization. These are folks who connect like William Dawes—with one large branch, rather than several branches of varying sizes. A narrow focus, with a single larger branch like Dawes, may have held one very big branch like the one on the left in my diagram. Meanwhile, all the other branches would be much smaller.

If, instead, you seek to cast as broad of a net as possible—more like Paul Revere, a "connector" or "elbow" of every deal—you want network maps with limited overlap. These types of networks, compared to my own, would have many more branches, even if there were fewer connections within each branch. The next time you recruit someone into your team, consider, where does their network map overlap your own and that of the team?

As for your existing connections, be sure to reinforce and strengthen those connections with frequent contact. Obama understood this and frequently contacted his base of supporters through multiple mediums. Whether it was video or micro-blogging posts, it seemed like the President was constantly in contact. Remember, it's not just about quantity of connections; quality matters as well.

Quantity *and* Quality

There is a never-ending debate over quality versus quantity in both social media and leadership circles. The right answer is both. Quantity matters insofar as, while it only takes a few passionate people to begin changing the world, eventually you need more people. However, quality matters because if you have a million people following you, but none of them actually read what you send, you will have no impact. We may not know the answer to this age-old question: "If a tree falls in a forest and no one is around to hear it, does it make a sound?" But we do know that, if content is distributed and nobody reads it, it makes no impact. To ensure your influence as a leader, your connections should reflect both quantity and quality.

Connect Recap

Connections were among the greatest strengths of colonial patriots. Their network was a great weakness of the British in their loyalist dependencies. Barack Obama and Jenny Lawson understood the power of connectivity and social media networks. Those on the losing end of these equations will be those who disrespect the power of connections. This is a mistake that I doubt BrandLink Communications will make again.

To be a great leader in the social media generation, you need to build your connections and respect those of others. One great way to build, strengthen, and sustain your own connections is by being open.

Open

The virtual walls that once surrounded our organizations no longer exist. Social media connections are opening the culture of teams to the world. As a result, leaders who relied upon the corporate veil, which enabled them to conduct one culture internally and present another to the world, struggle to maintain that façade. In contrast, leaders who always promoted positive cultures are reaping the benefits of their convictions. There have been instances of these great leaders since the beginning of time, but I'll start with the American Revolution examples.

John Hancock

All fifty-six men who signed the Declaration of Independence showed great courage. They were all open about their convictions. Announcing independence from Great Britain was an act of treason—a capital offense; nevertheless, many American patriots were undeterred from publishing their thoughts. These leaders were very candid and transparent—especially given the risks incurred by the authors and printers when the source was known. Yet these people all stood up for what they believed in and were brave enough to expose their convictions to oppressors.

John Hancock, in particular, is known for his famously large and bold signature. While popular belief maintains that Hancock signed boldly to ensure King George III could easily read his name, this fact is unfounded.[54]

To ensure your influence as a leader, your connections should reflect both quantity and quality.

Even so, Hancock still deserves credit for going first and signing boldly, as he did. In many ways, he led the Declaration of Independence by being the first to sign. Both his willingness to sign first and his large, bold signature reflect Hancock's principle of openness.

Thomas Paine's Open Publications

Thomas Paine's publications were highly regarded during the American Revolution. At critical points of low morale, Washington would read Paine's publications to rally his troops—and rally they did. In publishing his work, Paine took great risks, but remained very transparent with colonials. His publications included:

Common Sense (1776): Prior to *Common Sense*, publications arguing for independence all looked at the history of England and America. They always focused on what had happened in the past. *Common Sense* was the first document to look only to the future when considering whether colonists should break from Britain. This publication pondered what benefit England offered

America in the future rather than what it did in the past. It argued that independence was "common sense." That colonists had nothing to gain by remaining under the crown was a strong argument for revolution.

The American Crisis (1776–1783): A series of pamphlets that advocated for the revolution. These were popular reading and periodical motivation for colonial patriots.

In 1776, John Adams said of Thomas Paine's work,[55] "Without the pen of the author of *Common Sense*, the sword of Washington would have been raised in vain."

William Howe and Henry Clinton

Unlike colonial patriot soldiers who fought for their land and families, the British military was there mostly for their career. As a result, there were military leaders who weighed their decisions with a balance of what's best for the war against what's best for their careers. While the signers of the Declaration seemed to be chanting "All for one," British military leaders like William Howe and Henry Clinton seemed to chant "All for me." Two such scenarios resulted in Howe and Clinton being less than open about their intent with fellow commanding officers.

William Howe (British Commander)

General William Howe wanted to see Henry Clinton receive control of the Northern British armies in America. This was at least in part because he saw Clinton as less of a political threat than the other obvious option, General Burgoyne. Therefore, while occupying New York, Howe requested that control of the British's northern armies be given to Clinton.

Instead, control of the Northern armies was given to Burgoyne. This left Howe fearing the political power of his peer. As a result, when Burgoyne was to attack the colonial patriots down the Hudson River and join General Howe midway for reinforcement, Howe was scheming a self-serving ulterior plan.

As Burgoyne prepared his march down the Hudson, the Continental Congress of the colonial patriots abandoned Philadelphia. This left a largely symbolic opportunity for Howe. Yet attacking a relatively undefended Philadelphia meant abandoning Burgoyne. For the self-serving Howe, this was all the better.

As Burgoyne made his advance south from Montreal to take Albany and control the Hudson River, he expected reinforcement and support from Howe to the south. Howe never made it clear to Burgoyne that he did not intend to reinforce him or support his efforts. In fact, in a letter to Burgoyne, Howe alluded to an expectation that he would support Burgoyne:

> *"...be assured I shall soon be after (Washington) to relieve you."*—*Commander in Chief, General William Howe*

This letter suggested Howe would be available to support Burgoyne in his campaign down the Hudson. To the contrary, Howe sent his forces on a mission to conquer Philadelphia and abandoned Burgoyne.

The result was likely what Howe desired, if only in the very short-term. Namely, Burgoyne appeared to utterly fail in his campaign down the Hudson. This detracted from potential political and career competition for Howe from Burgoyne.

While Burgoyne was failing on the Hudson campaign, Howe successfully took Philadelphia, though at a substantial cost. Howe's concern for his own career over the best decisions for the British Empire prevented him from being entirely open about intentions.

Burgoyne surrendered his Northern army in October. This victory for the Americans bolstered support from France and officially engaged them in the war on the side of the colonial patriots. In total, Howe's failure to be open with his peers:

1. Cost the British their Northern armies
2. Lost the British an opportunity to control the Hudson River
3. Increased the opposition's forces by engaging France in the war

With support from France now assured to the colonists, Howe's control weakened. Consequently, Howe sent his letter of resignation to Great Britain later that same month.

Henry Clinton (British Commander)

Sir Henry Clinton succeeded General Howe as the British commander in chief. As a result, Clinton managed the military efforts of Britain during the latter years of the war. What Howe did to Burgoyne in the North, Clinton did to Cornwallis in the South.

Most of Clinton's directions regarding the New England colonies focused on maintaining existing British strongholds. Rather than advancing to conquer new ground, most of the effort was pushed south under Clinton's second-in-command, Lord Cornwallis.

Throughout the duration, Cornwallis reflected frustration for his lack of control and inability to maneuver in the South. In response to Cornwallis' reinforcement requests, Clinton was often insincere and noncommittal. According to Cornwallis,[56] Clinton restricted his ability to take decisive action, asserting instead that reinforcements were on the way; yet reinforcements did not come.

As Cornwallis hunkered down in Yorktown, he foresaw impending doom for his Southern campaign and potentially the whole British army in America. Cornwallis continued to call desperately for reinforcements, and Clinton said they would come as soon as possible.

Historians argue that Clinton could have sent troops sooner. Instead, it seems Clinton wanted Cornwallis to fail so that he could pin the blame for the faltering campaign squarely on his shoulders. Had Clinton either given more independence of control to Cornwallis or been open about the timing of reinforcements, perhaps Yorktown would not have fallen.

By the time troops shipped south, it was too late. The French had arrived to block reinforcements by sea and colonial forces had the land routes completely cut off. Cornwallis surrendered at Yorktown, marking the beginning of the end for Great Britain.

Whatever their reason, the failure of British military leaders to be open with each other and their men caused huge damage to their campaigns. When contrasted with the ability of American patriots to be remarkably open, it is clear how the open nature of leadership can help leaders succeed.

Today, being open with your team means ensuring that they understand your intentions, decisions, and support. Transparency with the team means that as the situation changes, they can respond in the best manner. Being open also means having nothing to hide. Clinton and Howe had plenty to hide, and that was the root of their downfall. Leaders with plenty to hide will fall quickly in today's world as well. On the other hand, leaders who expose the truth and remain open with their connections will strengthen their cause. In our contemporary example, this is a principle that brought Patrick Doyle success at Domino's Pizza.

Patrick Doyle

Imagine you are the president of Domino's Pizza. You love the company and brand, but there's an awful lot of bad press out there. A lot of people complain about poor quality, bad service, and other issues. What would you do? If you followed popular business and public relations advice, you would probably brush it under the rug and maybe work on one bad area at a time. After all, the company is profitable; why worry about it?

Not Patrick Doyle. Instead, he leads the "Oh Yes We Did!" campaign. In this campaign, Domino's marketing asks, "Did we actually face our critics and rebuild our pizza from the crust up? *Oh Yes We Did!*" The company actually sought out and compiled the negative feedback. Then they published the worst comments, photos, and complaints on a website they built to *highlight* the bad press.

Doyle then spearheaded the campaign. He went on camera and said, in essence:

We hear you. Our pizza's horrible. We're fixing it. Tell me if you find something wrong.

In presenting a candid face to the public, this corporate leader showed all his stakeholders that the company was listening and taking action. Mr. Doyle was also very open about the state of the business, product, and service. He left nothing to hide.

Domino's ability to admit failure, accept the need to change, and broadcast that to the world through social forums is an outstanding example of the open social principle. Unfortunately, most leaders today remain paralyzed by their legal departments and fears of being open. One such paralyzed leader is Mike Parry, the Minnesota State Senator.

Mike Parry

Where Doyle and Domino's took the opportunity to be completely open about their weaknesses, this Minnesota State Senator chose another path. When Mr. Parry realized he stood a good chance of winning the election, he began doing some "cleanup" work.

Parry decided to review his social media posts and look for anything that offended constituents, including one that read,[57] "Read the exclusive on Mr. O. in Newsweek. He is a power hungry Arrogant Black man." The article Parry referred to was, of course, on U.S. President Barack Obama.

Parry seemed to think his many followers and political pundits somehow didn't see that post—among others—and deleted them. When questioned on the offensive post, his answers varied.

Parry began by suggesting he never even sent the message. Later, he suggested he didn't even know how to delete posts. Then, as pressure built, he ultimately confessed to writing the post and deleting it, but downplayed the relevance of the matter.

Had Parry been open about posting and deleting the comment, there would have been little question on the matter. After all, most of us can relate to sending a message we regret and wanting to remove it later. However, because Senator Parry chose not to be open about the matter, his constituents must question his ability to be open in the future.

Openness Tools and Techniques

Being open is not easy for those who do not come by it naturally. That said, there are some techniques leaders can use to avoid mistakes.

It starts with the simple reminder, don't say or do anything you wouldn't want published on the front page of the paper tomorrow. Otherwise, you run the risk of backpedaling or defending a position you never intended to support. This is obvious when we're in the right state of mind. However, there are times to be especially cautious of risks:

Long Days
Long days at the office make us especially susceptible to bad decisions. If you are tired, you are more likely to cave to a bad idea. Long days, along with the physical and mental duress associated with them, have been blamed for many bad decisions.

High Stress
When under a great deal of pressure, you may say or do something out of frustration. A classic example of this was when British Petroleum's (BP) then CEO Tony Hayward, facing the worst oil spill in U.S. History, infuriated stakeholders with his comment:[58] "There's no one who wants this thing over more than I do, I'd like my life back." News of Hayward's self-centered focus spread like wildfire on social channels.

Chemical Influence
Whether they are over-the-counter, prescription, or otherwise, chemicals influence our judgment. Be aware of this, and, if you can't avoid it altogether, set guidelines regarding when to conduct business and when not to. If you're socializing after hours, keep it social.

You may not be able to avoid all these situations, but be aware of the impact they may have on your judgment. Then set expectations accordingly. Furthermore, consider how each decision you make could be interpreted. Ask yourself the following questions:

1. Am I being honest?
2. Am I manipulating words to mask reality?

3. If stakeholders make commitments based on this, will it help or hurt them?
4. What does my gut tell me?

Don't underestimate that last question. Your gut knows reality. If you feel uncertain of what you are communicating, and your gut is telling you as much, you're not being open. If you're open with your communications, you're less likely to regret it later than if you act like Howe, Clinton, or Parry.

Open Recap

From American patriots in the Revolution, you can see how being open can win over thousands—especially when being open is a matter of life or death. While Patrick Doyle and Domino's did not face such a life-threatening matter, they showed how being open in business can also win over stakeholders.

These were lessons the British and Senator Mike Parry failed to heed. The results were disastrous for the British, ultimately leading to their demise in the American Revolution. While Mike Parry did win a seat in the Senate, one wonders how much his lack of openness cost him—both literally and figuratively.

The open nature of an individual may be critical for one more reason: it points to the degree to which that leader serves their organization. One who is open about their motivation and intent is likely focused on serving others. In contrast, the leader who conceals reality and intent is likely more focused on self-serving concerns. After all, if a leader has your best interest at heart, what could he have to hide?

Serve

Finally, we get to the heart of the matter. Do you serve your stakeholders or yourself? If you're not serving others, you're not leading anyone. Service is truly the core of the matter when it comes to leadership. Unfortunately, the term "leadership" has become misunderstood by so many that we need a term to clarify its definition. Those who comprehend what leadership really is advocate "Servant Leadership." For the colonial patriots, we look to George Washington as an example of Servant Leadership.

George Washington

George Washington epitomized Servant Leadership during his role as commander in chief in more ways than we can cover here. However, below are a few highlights.

To begin with, George Washington accepted his role as commander in chief of the Continental Army under the condition that he could serve without pay. Throughout his entire service during the war, Washington drew no salary and only saw his expenses reimbursed.[59]

Washington also never asked anything of his men that he was not willing to do himself. He served with them, fought alongside them, and grew old in service with them. This was exemplified in the Newburgh Address. Many officers were threatening mutiny over Congress's failure to pay them. To dissuade them and prevent the effective abandonment of the war, Washington stumbled over several words while trying to read a letter to the officers. He pulled out his spectacles and said, "Gentlemen, you must pardon me. I have grown gray in your service and now find myself growing blind." According to many accounts,[60] the officers were so moved at their dedicated, empathetic leader, that many began to weep.

Washington also showed resolve beyond his personal health sacrifice. How else can you define the man who took on the responsibility of leading a couple thousand untrained men against the most efficient and powerful military force in the world? Washington was resolute in his commitment to the colonies and their vision for independence. But it wasn't only his service to the people as military leader that revealed his resolve; it was also his resignation. When the war was over, many people, including King George, expected Washington to assume the power of first leader of the nation through his military control. When King George was informed that Washington intended to resign his post and all that power, the King said,[61] "If he does that he will be the greatest man in the world." Washington did just that and only returned to political office as our first president at the demand of the people, months later.

In reality, many of the colonial patriots could be used as an example of great Servant Leadership. On the other side, many British leaders could be used to exemplify failures of Servant Leadership. For our purposes, though, I'll look at the failings of King George himself.

King George III

In response to the Declaration of Rights, King George summarized his perspective by stating that ". . . the Colonies must either submit or triumph." [62] His perspective was unyielding to the needs of colonial patriots. The perspective of the King, Parliament, and British leadership was not to serve the men and women of America, but to control and contain them.

In the colonial era, the people had limited power to demand service from their leaders and resorted to military force. Today, through the power of social media, Servant Leadership is demanded more than ever before.

Social media advocates explain that one of its many benefits is the ability to empower people's "trash filter." Actually, they use another term, but you get the idea. I believe this is accurate. Thanks to social media, corporate marketing trash sticks out like a sore thumb. If you're not genuinely interested in and concerned about your stakeholders, they see it. Your stakeholders see through corporate jargon and profiteering. They see through it because:

- You're not interested in connecting through social media.
- Your only message in social media is sales.
- You only monitor social media when convenient.
- You're not practicing the principles in this book.

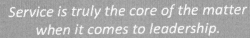

Service is truly the core of the matter when it comes to leadership.

If serving your stakeholders is not a priority, your stakeholders will know and quickly lose interest. At the heart of your culture, therefore, should be a desire to serve and to serve first. Many of the examples that I've covered above are great at serving others, but the example I'd like to highlight here is Tony Hsieh, the CEO of digital retailer Zappos.com.[63]

Tony Hsieh

Zappos.com employees will tell you they are a service company that just happens to sell products. I recently had the opportunity to meet the Zappos.com Insights team and tour their Las Vegas headquarters. I assure you, they are a company that focuses on serving others first.

When you first enter their office building, above the front desk is a large sign that reads, "Powered by Service." Service to the customer is paramount. For leaders in the company, like CEO Tony Hsieh, service to the employees is also a top priority. For example, the company provides free food to employees.

More impressive, they also provide personal coaching services. In fact, they have a staircase containing the "Culture Wall" where employees list the goals they've achieved. The employees can either sign their achievements on the wall or leave them anonymous. Examples on that wall range from, "I achieved (an outstanding) professional recognition," to "I became a better dad," and even "I increased my biceps by two inches!"

As for the customers, there are hundreds of great stories. Just a couple include:

- One customer called with no interest in buying a product, but wanted directions to the nearest pizza store. The Zappos.com employee obliged by looking it up and giving directions.
- Another customer, after returning a pair of unused shoes that were purchased by a recently deceased relative, received flowers at the funeral from Zappos.com.
- Other employees are known to listen for hours to callers who are just lonely and want to talk. The record for duration, with no purchase, is now over eight hours.

Zappos.com understands what it means to serve first. Tony and the leadership team at Zappos.com established the culture of serving employees first. The employees in turn pass along that service to the customers. In serving the customers, Zappos.com employees also serve their shareholders.

These stakeholders, thrilled by the commitment to service they see in Zappos.com, spread the word. Speak to a Zappos.com customer, and it will be hard not to hear a story of great service. These stakeholders are reviewing products and services online as well. This all adds up to measurable proof that some companies are better to do business with than others.

Automated systems index reviews and publish scores for any potential customer to see. Want to buy a pair of boots online? Within three clicks you will know which company has the best price and which company offers the best service. If Zappos.com is close on price, you bet they get the sale because their service is stellar. Take this as an example:

You're going to your best friend's wedding, and you need a new pair of shoes to go with that great dress (guys, bear with me here). You look online and find the perfect match. After typing in the shoe brand, style, and size, you are immediately presented three stores that sell the shoe. All three stores are within about three dollars of each other on price. Next to each store you see:

1. Customer Service Ratings
2. Number of Customers Rating
3. Highlights of the Best and Worst Reviews for Each

The first store is the least expensive at $29.50 for the pair of shoes. However, it only has 2.5 out of 5 stars for customer service. Furthermore, only eight people have reviewed their service. One highlighted customer review reads, "Price was right, service was slow, and one shoe had a scuff mark on it!"

The second store is slightly more expensive at $30.95. However, fifty-three people reviewed their customer service and gave them a 4 out of 5. Their highlighted review reads, "Good price and friendly service, but they charge extra for two-day delivery."

Finally, Zappos.com shows 4.9 out 5 stars. Yes, their price is the most expensive, but only slightly so at $31.95. Over three hundred people have reviewed them. The highlighted comment reads, "Service was amazing! They offered free 2 day delivery and even included a free return shipping envelope in case they didn't fit!"

Which company sounds more interested in serving their customers? Which company would you buy from?

It is through their focus on serving all their stakeholders that Zappos.com reflects great service in social media and generates sustainable fiscal success. Unfortunately, Bob Nardelli, the former CEO of Home Depot and Chrysler, did not understand the importance of serving *all* stakeholders.

Bob Nardelli

Bob Nardelli first came to business fame at General Electric, where he studied under the infamous policies of Jack Welch. These policies included the "up or out," or "20-70-10" approach to employee management. In this system, [64] employees are force-ranked, and each year, leadership is encouraged to fire the bottom ten percent of employees.

This focus on firing ten percent of employees every year was largely perceived as a focus on shareholders at the expense of employees. Years later, GE itself is pulling away from this management methodology.[65] Nonetheless, Nardelli took this exclusive focus on shareholders with him to Home Depot after being passed over for the CEO job at GE.

Here's one example of how Nardelli tried to apply these management concepts: he set out to replace the entrepreneurial culture of Home Depot with a pure management-by-numbers approach. He also eliminated many executive positions and reduced the number of skilled in-store staff.

It didn't stop there. Another symbol of his lack of interest in employees, Nardelli had nine parking spaces reserved for him[66] at the Home Depot headquarters. The elevator he used then took him straight to his penthouse office, without stopping on any floors. Nardelli's clear lack of service to the consumer and employees offended many insiders.

At the same time Nardelli made these cuts in customer service and employee support, Home Depot's chief competitor, Lowe's, *expanded* its emphasis on customer service. Given a choice of stores to shop at, customers therefore chose Lowe's. This meant that, over time, Home Depot sales declined. Given a choice of companies to work for, skilled employees chose the one with a greater investment in their people. Therefore, employee skills, morale, and commitment at Home Depot declined.

Bob Nardelli executed an emphasis on serving the investors at the exclusion of all other stakeholders. This approach often appeals to executives because it achieves near-term gains, boosts their compensation, and recognizes the executive as accountable for improving the company's market share. However, the failure to serve all stakeholders hurts the company in the long-term. Through social media, this is more apparent than ever before. Social media exposes one-trick ponies that hide in ivory towers.

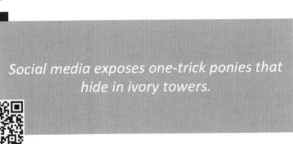

Social media exposes one-trick ponies that hide in ivory towers.

As consumers and employees share ratings and complaints on social media platforms, the shaky ground on which fiscal results are built becomes apparent. Executives who could get away with these short-term methods can no longer mask the overall damage left in their wake. This formerly possible solution was an easy formula:

Cut Costs to the Bone + Boost Sales Through Incentives + Exit Before the Piper Must be Paid = Success

Now, costs that were cut to the bone are exposed on the butcher block of social media platforms. Disgruntled employees post management reviews on public forums, and unhappy consumers post negative reviews. And an exit before the piper must be paid? Forget about it.

The old world forgot about the damages when it came time to the pay the piper. The social media world does not forget so easily. In fact, stakeholders talk as the rats flee the sinking ship. No longer is stock price the only measurable feedback available to the public.

Executives who fail to focus on serving all stakeholders will fail to lead successfully. Social media knocks down the firewall that hides these cracks in the foundation of an organization. If you want to succeed in the social media revolution, serve your stakeholders—all of them.

> *Now, costs that were cut to the bone are exposed on the butcher block of social media platforms.*

Servant Leadership Tools and Techniques

Servant Leadership entails a focus on serving first through leadership. In other words, the servant leader desires to help their stakeholders, so they serve those stakeholders. As time passes, the individual comes to realize they can best serve their stakeholders by leading them.[67]

That is the embodiment of Servant Leadership: a leader who seeks to serve first, desires to serve all stakeholders, and chooses to serve them through leadership. Anything else is not leadership, but self-service.

Traditional leadership philosophy—particularly in business—is opposed to Servant Leadership. In most organizations, leaders seek the official position of leader for the benefits it offers. These benefits range from compensation to title. Executives desire the admiration of their peers and the publicity and fame from outsiders. Leadership is often misunderstood as an accomplishment to be reached, rather than a commitment to serve. This is where the term "leadership" has run ashore on the rocky reefs of pride.

Flip the Pyramid

Leadership is traditionally pictured using a pyramid, with the leader at the top and the stakeholders at various levels below. For example, the leader would be placed at the tip of the pyramid, with employees at the next level down, and consumers below employees. This pyramid suggests that each level below supports the level above. Consumers, purchasing products, support employee compensation. Employees, in turn, support the decisions executed by the leader.

Servant Leadership is often depicted visually as the same pyramid, flipped on its head. In other words, instead of consumers meeting the needs of employees, who serve the leader, the reverse is true. The leader serves the needs of employees, who in turn serve the needs of consumers.

Social media technology strengthens the ability for leaders to flip the pyramid. It is easier than ever for leaders to have direct conversations with all stakeholder groups. In fact, all stakeholder groups are even easier to hear. Leaders who can listen to stakeholders more effectively understand those stakeholders. With better understanding comes a greater ability to serve.

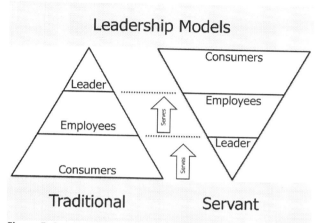

Figure 5: Servant Leadership vs. traditional pyramids

In effect, everyone has a megaphone, and no one can be denied a voice. Therefore, stakeholders demand greater service from their leaders. They're using their megaphones to ensure they're heard, and they're not going away until they are served.

Without Serving, You're not Leading

The leader who serves others leads them. The leader who serves self-interest leads none.

> *"He that thinketh he leadeth and hath no one following him is only taking a walk."* —John C. Maxwell

As Maxwell points out—those with no followers are not leading. The saying can be easily extended to those with controlled or forced followers. If someone is obligated to follow you for compensation, security, or other reasons they deem a necessity, they are not truly following. Instead, those "followers" are a form of dependent.

If you desire to be a leader—forget it, you're not ready. If, instead, you want to serve and believe you can serve most effectively as a leader, then you get it. Lead by serving your stakeholders.

> Leadership is often misunderstood as an accomplishment to be reached, rather than a commitment to serve.

In a world of openness and transparency, your followers see the difference between leaders with self-interest and those serving others. Therefore, focus on service—not leadership. Through service, the leadership will come naturally. If you're serving stakeholders, you will be yourself and find yourself in the right role, at the right organization with the right culture. Through service, your followers, stakeholders, and team will desire your leadership.

Why the Term Servant

Many executives wrestle with the term Servant Leadership. The term servant, itself, disturbs many people otherwise advocating these principles. For example, in the landmark work, *Good to Great*,[68] Jim Collins explains how his team almost used the term "Servant Leader" instead of "Level 5 Leader," but feared it would be misinterpreted.

Here are some of the common misconceptions leading to these objections and the rebuttals:

- **Servant Implies Slavery:** The misconception is that the term "servant" means the same as "slave." This is not true. In truth, slavery implies a sense of being owned by others.

  Rebuttal: Servant implies service to others. Servant Leadership is not slavery, and the leader is not owned by those they serve. The leader makes a conscious choice to serve. They are not forced.

- **Servant Implies Subservience:** Subservient behavior implies unquestioning support. The argument is that a Servant Leader is subservient and would therefore do anything the people wanted. The fear being that the leader would be easily convinced of many bad decisions.

  Rebuttal: Servant Leadership is not unquestioning support. In order to effectively serve others, you must sometimes do what is unpopular with followers. There is nothing subservient in that.

- **Focus on Followers:** Many opponents of Servant Leadership think these leaders serve only their followers. For nonprofits, this could mean a focus on the employees over those the organization is meant to serve. For business, this could mean a focus on the employees over the shareholders.

  Rebuttal: The truth is a Servant Leader must focus on serving all stakeholders. These include followers, employees, customers, partners, investors, the community, and more. A leader who serves one group and not the others is not a Servant Leader.

- **Religious Concept:** Many people believe Servant Leadership is a religious concept. Secular organizations, especially the public sector of business, are therefore afraid of advocating a "religious" concept at work.

Rebuttal: As a Christian, I am proud of the fact that Servant Leadership principles are taught throughout The Bible. A similar perspective exists across most major religions. However, the concept of Servant Leadership itself is secular in nature. Friend and Servant Leadership advocate Larry Spears once framed it well for me: [69] "Servant Leadership transcends religion."

Whatever the reason, most opponents of the term Servant Leadership have at least one of these misconceptions. Whatever your perspective, it is important to get the facts. Jim Collins was afraid people would have false preconceived notions. Here's hoping this concern is not proliferated.

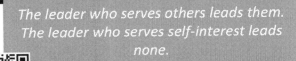

The leader who serves others leads them. The leader who serves self-interest leads none.

In contrast to those objecting to the term, here's why I insist on using the term Servant:

- **Paradox:** Leadership is a paradox of responsibilities. Your accountabilities require you to make decisions and create influence, often from afar. Yet you cannot ask your stakeholders to do anything which you are not willing to do yourself. To sustain the support of your team, you must always be willing to jump into the fray yourself. What could be a better way to capture this essence than in the paradox of the term "Servant Leader"?

- **Shock Factor:** Indeed, there is a degree of shock and awe in this term. We need it. For too long, too many people have associated leadership with achievement. It is not achievement; it is a commitment to serve. This factor, combined with the plethora of books claiming to be on leadership, demands a rude awakening—a tough love, if you will. The term "servant" helps shake people out of their comfort zone.

- **Definition:** The very definition of the term is in the name. When people say leadership is hard to define, I disagree. Leadership is leadership. The term "servant" is only necessary because too many people have been led astray to believe leadership does not include service.

> *To sustain the support of your team, you must always be willing to jump into the fray yourself.*

Those conflicted on the term "servant" should consider why we continue to use the term. After all, the growing number of adopters could just as easily select another book-of-the-month term for their leadership and avoid the many questions around "servant." Why do we persist, and why is the Servant Leadership movement growing? Because it is the heart of true leadership, and people want real leaders—not show ponies.

Traditional Models of Servant Leadership

The term Servant Leadership was coined by former AT&T executive Robert K. Greenleaf in "The Servant as Leader."[70] In this essay, Greenleaf said:

"The servant-leader is servant first . . . It begins with the natural feeling that one wants to serve, to serve first. Then conscious choice brings one to aspire to lead. That person is sharply different from one who is leader first, perhaps because of the need to assuage an unusual power drive or to acquire material possessions . . . The leader-first and the servant-first are two extreme types.

"The difference manifests itself in the care taken by the servant-first to make sure that other people's highest priority needs are being served. The best test, and difficult to administer, is: Do those served grow as persons? Do they, while being served, become healthier, wiser, freer, more autonomous, more likely themselves to become servants? And, what is the effect on the least privileged in society? Will they benefit or at least not be further deprived?"

While Greenleaf coined the term when this essay was published in 1970, we can see these principles of Servant Leadership in practice throughout history. As a result, there have been many different models of Servant Leadership. The most popular models, though, are the Christian and the Greenleaf/Spears models.

Christian Model

As we discussed earlier, the concept of Servant Leadership is a secular one. However, most major world religions have their own take on what Servant Leadership means for their followers. There are both Jewish and Islamic blogs that discuss the concept and advocate Servant Leadership principles, but the world religion with the most prevalent position on this is Christianity.

Christianity, my own faith, looks to Jesus of Nazareth as our Lord and Savior. His example on earth was the ultimate example of Servant Leadership. The humility and service of Jesus were godly. Biblical verses that point to Servant Leadership for Christians include (New International Version):

> **John 13:12-15:** "When he had finished washing their feet, he put on his clothes and returned to his place. 'Do you understand what I have done for you?' he asked them. 'You call me "Teacher" and "Lord," and rightly so, for that is what I am. Now that I, your Lord and Teacher, have washed your feet, you also should wash one another's feet. I have set you an example that you should do as I have done for you.'"

> **Matthew 20:26-28**: "Not so with you. Instead, whoever wants to become great among you must be your servant, and whoever wants to be first must be your slave—just as the Son of Man did not come to be served, but to serve, and to give his life as a ransom for many."

> **Philippians 2:3-8**: "Do nothing out of selfish ambition or vain conceit. Rather, in humility value others above yourselves, not looking to your own interests but each of you to the interests of the others.

> In your relationships with one another, have the same mindset as Christ Jesus:

> Who, being in very nature God, did not consider equality with God something to be used to his own advantage;

> rather, he made himself nothing by taking the very nature of a servant, being made in human likeness.

> And being found in appearance as a man, he humbled himself by becoming obedient to death—even death on a cross!"

These verses, among others, and the life and example of Jesus Christ reflect the call for Servant Leadership for Christians. If you're Christian, it's actually hard to argue for any other form of leadership.

Greenleaf / Spears Model

The Greenleaf Center for Servant Leadership has been an amazing resource for spreading Servant Leadership awareness. As such, the bulk of references to Servant Leadership point back to the quotes I covered earlier and use this model for describing the philosophy.

Larry Spears was the CEO of the Greenleaf Center for nearly twenty years and now runs the Spears Center for Servant Leadership. His extensive research on Robert Greenleaf's writings drove his framing of the Greenleaf model into the Ten Characteristics of Servant Leadership. [71] Through ModernServantLeader.com, I categorized these ten characteristics into three focus-areas: Servant, Leadership, and the combined Servant Leadership. These characteristics include:

Servant	Leadership	Servant Leadership
Listening	Awareness	Stewardship
Empathy	Persuasion	Commitment to People
Healing	Conceptualization	Building Community
	Foresight	

I am often asked to describe Servant Leadership. In our culture today, people desire elegant simplicity. As mentioned earlier, this is one reason I am partial to the term Servant Leadership: it is self-descriptive. Still, I found it difficult to really explain Servant Leadership in a concise manner with the existing models. Therefore, I came up with the following acronym model.

Acronym Model of Servant Leadership

> "If I have seen further it is by standing on the shoulders of giants." —Sir Isaac Newton

Servant Leadership advocates today truly stand on the shoulders of giants. However, to spread awareness and adoption of these principles for leaders in the social media revolution, we must be perceived as more relevant than historic models.

More Relevant Than Ever

Of course, my job of making Servant Leadership more relevant is easy in this world of social media. The ease with which individuals organize around issues is greater than ever before. Therefore, organizations' need for greater leadership is frequently being raised through social media channels.

The power shift we covered earlier leaves people demanding different and better leadership. This also leaves leaders scratching their heads when the autocratic, top-down leadership practices of the industrial revolution fail them.

These changes in our culture are obvious to many. As a result, many people seek something new and better when it comes to leadership. The irony is that what we want and what we need has been in front of us all along. It is Servant Leadership and, while it dates back to early history, it is more in demand today than ever before.

The irony is that what we want and what we need has been in front of us all along.

The Servant Leadership Acronym Model is really just a mash-up of so many predecessors. In keeping with the elegant simplicity perspective, Servant Leadership is the following acronym:

Selfless
Empathetic
Resolute
Virtuous
Authentic
Nascent
Thorough

As I cover these concepts below, I often refer back to the Spears Model. This is because the Spears Model is the most frequently referenced model and connects us to the origin of the Servant Leadership term. As a result, this shows a consistency across definitions and grounds my forward-looking model in the best of our past.

Selfless

Earlier, I said that if you're not serving, you're not leading. This captures the selfless nature of leadership in a simple statement. Selflessness is about putting the needs of others before yourself. Specifically, we speak here of putting the needs of those you serve first. In the Spears model, he captured this by including values such as humility, listening, stewardship, building community, and commitment to people.

Empathetic

In order to lead another person, you need to know what it feels like to walk a mile in their shoes. Even if you've never been in their position yourself, you must have the empathy to perceive their circumstances. This is why so many corporate leaders like Bob Nardelli, who distance themselves from those they serve, lose the commitment of their people. Leaders who lose the ability to empathize lose the ability to lead. In the

Spears model, key attributes of empathy also included healing, awareness, and persuasion.

Resolute

The resolve of a leader is often overlooked in traditional Servant Leadership perspectives, yet it is a critical attribute of effective Servant Leaders. As Tony Hsieh and revolutionary leaders of all types faced detractors, it would have been easy to say, "we don't really need a unique culture" or "it'd be easier to give into the British directive." If they had done that, nothing would have changed. Servant Leaders must be resolute in their mission and actions.

Virtuous

Character and integrity are more important today than ever. People have always demanded leaders to be virtuous. Today, failures of character are identified, documented, and shared at the speed of a keystroke. It's well-documented that people love to see powerful leaders fall. Nothing undermines a leader's mission faster than a failure of his or her character. Stakeholders don't want leaders who are only good at their job; they demand leaders who represent what is best in all of us. The well-rounded leader is one with strong virtues.

Authentic

If being virtuous is about constantly embodying moral qualities, authenticity is about proving the practice of those qualities to your stakeholders. To serve others effectively, you must be transparent about actions and intentions. This authenticity is demanded by stakeholders. If you want loyalty and commitment from others, they must know that you are candid, sincere about your intentions, and opposed to practicing dirty politics. If a follower is uncertain about your intent, they will not convert. If they think your primary objective is increased sales and revenues rather than mutual benefit, forget about their buying from you.

The well-rounded leader is one with strong virtues.

Nascent

Organizations are constantly changing, whether for better or worse. In order for organizations to thrive, their leaders must always be on the lookout for great new ideas. This is why Servant Leaders must be open-minded. Great leaders understand that great ideas may come from anywhere. The people closest to the problem are often the ones best prepared to find a solution—not the senior executive, who hasn't been on the front lines in a decade. Therefore, Servant Leaders realize they must constantly grow and evolve, listening to the requirements and contributions of their stakeholders. As Darwin Smith, CEO of the "good" turned "great" company Kimberly-Clark, said,[72] *"I never stopped trying to become qualified for the job."*

Thorough

A major failure of leaders today is an emphasis on short-term benefits without regard for the long-term costs. This trade-off, to make themselves and their results look great while pushing the costs and impact downstream, weakens institutions everywhere. In contrast, Servant Leaders are extremely thorough.

It may seem less exciting, but communications by Servant Leaders are very clear on what trade-offs must be made. Servant Leaders do not micromanage, but they do ensure that the leaders they put in place are equally thorough. Servant Leaders maximize the sustainability of results. This sustainability of results requires a great deal of planning for the future.

These results must also consider all stakeholders—not just a subset. For example, we cannot favor investors at the excessive cost of employees. In the Spears model of Servant Leadership, he highlights the thorough attributes of conceptualization and foresight.

Serve Recap

This is a simplification of a major concept. Great leadership is Servant Leadership. Now, more than ever, thanks to the evolution of social media, Servant Leadership is demanded from stakeholders. If this is the first time you've heard of Servant Leadership, I encourage further reading for your benefit. Until then, remember to be Selfless, Empathetic, Resolute, Virtuous, Authentic, Nascent, and Thorough.

Your Principles Summary

Wow, this was a long section, but it is the heart of this book. At the end of the day, you can have all the technology in the world, and it won't matter a bit because without a core of great leadership principles, you will not succeed as a leader. Likewise, you could have amazing leadership principles, but without applying them with the most effective tools today, you will be overshadowed by a lesser leader.

The Principles
> Listen
> Action-Oriented
> Integrity
> Connect
> Open
> Serve
>
> > (SERVANT: Selfless, Empathetic, Resolute, Virtuous, Authentic, Nascent, Thorough)

Reflection

1. Which principles are your strongest?
2. Which principles could you strengthen?
3. How will you strengthen your weakest principles?

YOUR ORGANIZATION

"A dream you dream alone is only a dream. A dream you dream together is reality."
—John Lennon

This book's primary focus is how to better serve your organization with leadership in the social media generation. Therefore, I've focused on individual leadership. That said, in my conversations with leaders, the discussion often turns to an inquiry on the organization itself. Questions like:

- What teams are most impacted by social media?
- What policies and procedures should we have?
- How do we avoid a social media crisis?

I want to cover some of these basics for you here . . .

Stages of Change

If your organization is not effectively engaged in social media leadership, you need to first understand that there is a lot of change ahead. You cannot simply turn on a switch and suddenly have everyone on the same page. There are stages of change you must go through. Here are the stages and how they relate to the adoption of social media leadership.

Behavioral psychologists have this big fancy term for how people make changes in their life. It's called "Transtheoretical Model of Behavior Change."[73] We'll just call it "Stages of Change." In essence, this is how people progress from denying a need to change through to a successful change of the behavior.

These stages of change are often referenced when describing the behavior of recovering drug addicts. However, they are also relevant when it comes to leadership in the social media generation. Many leaders, who resist the adoption of social media, also need to evolve through these stages.

You could be at any point in these stages yourself. Or you could be helping someone else through their stages of change. As you read through these stages of change, think about your organization as a whole. What is your current stage in the change process? Which leaders in your team need each of these steps? How can a great leader effect this change in your culture?

Stage 1: Precontemplation (Denial or "Not Ready to Change")

This is the denial phase. In precontemplation, we're saying there's no real issue here. Drug addicts still say, "I can quit whenever I want." Leaders say, "Social media is just a fad." What is needed here is an intervention. We need to break the cycle of denial. Drug addicts need their family to confront them. Leaders' peers need to show them how they will lose market share, revenue, and/or support from the team if they do not engage in social media.

Stage 2: Contemplation (Acceptance or "Getting Ready to Change")

Addicts admit that they have a problem, but have not yet committed to solving it. Leaders admit that the perceptions of their people are shifting, but aren't quite sure they must change themselves. During this stage, addicts need support of friends and family to grow their interest in changing. Leaders need the same: peers and team members to help educate and reinforce the growing awareness of social media.

Stage 3: Preparation (Committed or "Ready to Change")

Addicts have stopped seeing the dealer, but haven't gotten rid of their stash yet and may be weaning themselves off before quitting completely. Leaders are likely dabbling in social media, following their kids on the latest platform (to their children's chagrin), or perhaps reading blogs and books on Servant Leadership and social media principles. What is needed here includes examples, tools, and techniques. Addicts join a program or commit to a process. Leaders, likewise, need a routine—perhaps a schedule, monitoring suite, or training program.

Stage 4: Action (Initiating or "Starting to Change")

Addicts take it one day at a time—without the substance. Leaders have a social media account and are changing their behavior. Support is key. For an addict, a sponsor who keeps supporting and checking in with the addict through the most difficult days is vital. For a leader, this is likely the role of a mentor. Temptation to relapse is greatest as an addict and leader have recently changed their behaviors. As these temptations to relapse arise, a leader needs support.

Stage 5: Maintenance (Continuation or "Sustaining the Change")

An addict's been clean a while, and a leader's behavior is solidly changed. Still, temptations are likely to arise, though less frequently. It's in this stage that an addict's sponsor and a leader's mentor may not be around as often and, therefore, strong temptations for relapse are an even greater risk. An addict and leader need to depend upon themselves more, but the sponsor and mentor need to answer their call quickly, if needed.

You may already be past stages one and two. Perhaps you're preparing to help another leader for their change at an earlier point in the process. Whatever the case, be aware of the ever-present risk of relapse and the critical roles of peers and mentors.

Empowering Through Policies and Training

If you're setting out to control your employees with policies and procedures, gently close this book and put it back on the shelf. I can't help you.

Policies and procedures are not for "controlling" when it comes to social media and great leadership. Instead, it's about enabling, empowering, and informing your people so they can make the best decisions. Here's how you can do that with policies and procedures.

Tony Hsieh, CEO of Zappos.com, got it right when he set their communications policy (as I mentioned above) to simply, *"Be real and use your best judgment."* First, he didn't create a separate policy just for social media. Second, he kept the policy simple and clear for everyone to understand.

Of course, not everyone in your organization will be in favor of such elegant simplicity for your policies. Lawyers will tell you to define many scenarios and consider all the different angles you may be sued. At least, that's what most good lawyers will do—that's their job. So ask yourself, do you want a culture of fear against lawsuits or empowerment through leadership? Sure, the two may be able to coexist in perfect balance, but I've not seen it yet. Most great organizations lean heavily toward empowerment through leadership, with a dash of fear against lawsuits sprinkled in.

As guiding principles, here's how I'd suggest you look at policies for social media:

1. Expand on existing policies; don't create new ones.
2. Focus on your intent and aim at empowering, enabling, and informing employees—not controlling them.
3. Share them with employees. Encourage regular reviews of the policy.
4. Get input from the teams most impacted by the policies—what would they like to see as options?
5. If it's long, explain the objective of a policy at the start. An example may be, "This policy helps us ensure we're all on the same page."

> *Most great organizations lean heavily toward empowerment through leadership, with a dash of fear against lawsuits sprinkled in.*

Sample Communication Policy

Below is a sample communication policy, which encompasses social media, that you may find appropriate.

DISCLAIMER: *I am not a lawyer. The following is not legal advice.*

The objective of our communications policy is to ensure that we all represent our company in an appropriate, candid, and positive perspective. When in doubt, or if you have any questions, please contact our corporate relations manager, Jane Doe, at <insert phone number here>.

Disclosure

In any communication, written or verbal, about our company, products, and services, please disclose your relationship to the company. You must also mention that your opinions are your own. A good example is putting something like the following in any profile or biography: I work for ACME Company. Opinions are my own.

Positive Focus

We want our employees to be candid. That said, we also live by something our mother taught us, "If you haven't got something nice to say, don't say anything at all." Therefore, we ask that you try to reflect on the best aspects of our company, people, products, and services. If you have something critical to say, be sure to share in a constructive manner.

Remember, any conduct we find inappropriate or offensive to the reputation of our company could be grounds for termination.

Name Calling

Along with the emphasis on candor comes a need for sensitivity surrounding the industry. Please avoid name-calling of our competitors. In fact, it's best not to reference specific competitors. Instead, if you feel compelled to make a reference to others in our field, please use a generic reference, such as "the competitors."

Official Representation

If you are asked to offer an official perspective on behalf of our organization, please contact the corporate relations manager (name and number above) before offering any such perspective.

This policy is only one example. You must tailor your own as appropriate for your industry and people. Most importantly though, you need to empower and enable your people with these tools. Each role in your organization may need something slightly different as job descriptions, responsibilities, and roles evolve to adjust to the new landscape.

Personal or Professional Account

As your employees look to engage on social media, one big question is whether you encourage them to use their own personal accounts or create separate, professional accounts. As you might expect, the answer is that it depends. I generally recommend one of three scenarios:

Official Accounts

If the employee's job responsibilities include operating an official account for the company, brand, or product, you should create a separate, official account. There are several reasons for an official account:

1. **It's Official**: What comes from this account is supposed to be the voice of the brand, not necessarily the individual operating it.

2. **Multiple Operators**: These accounts often have more than one person using the account. This is especially true if the account is operated 24/7.

3. **Continuity**: As employees come and go, there remains a continuity of this account. You don't lose the account's connections with each new employee operating it.

Remember, it is important to have separate devices for official accounts. Several failures I have mentioned here—including Obama's Dead Grandmother, Chrysler's Detroit Drivers, and others—could have been avoided with separation of devices. In other words, whoever operates an official account must be well trained to separate that account from their personal accounts. The benefit of doing so is maximum clarity on which device, account, and communication is for work only.

Even if you use both the other scenarios below, it's a good idea to have an official account. Therefore, you should setup and operate an official account for each organization, brand, or product. If it's not used actively, though, be sure and point people to the active accounts.

Professional Accounts

Many organizations prefer to assign employees a professional account. For example, I could have an account such as @Ben_KatysHomeAppliances. This would identify me as an individual employee of Katy's Home Appliances. In this scenario, you can decide whether you still prefer employees to disclaim their posts as their own opinions or as the official word of the organization. What you decide here is determined by the employee's responsibilities and your policies.

Professional accounts work well when you have many employees with official responsibilities in social media platforms. However, I'm not as big of a fan of these. Instead, I prefer to simply encourage employees to use their own, personal accounts.

Personal Accounts

The most personal, authentic, and transparent way for your employees to engage with consumers on social media is through their own accounts. This is best represented as an analogy between the mask and the telephone.

> **Mask**: You would not ask your employees to wear a mask when speaking with customers or other stakeholders. So why would you ask them to use a separate account?

> **Telephone**: At the same time, you would not require employees to use their personal phone numbers when dealing with stakeholders on the behalf of the business. Therefore, you should not require employees to use their personal accounts.

I, for one, often give my personal phone number to customers, contractors, and other stakeholders of the company. This is because I am "all in." I am committed to the company, brands, and stakeholders that I serve. I only speak highly of them and therefore am not afraid to share my personal contact information. Still, not every employee is like this.

Employees who are proud of the organization and fully engaged are the best to have using personal accounts on social media for the organization. You should not require them to, but you should empower and enable them to do so. Remember your policies and training, though. Still ask them to disclaim their opinions as their own to protect the organization. Just don't block them from being personable, authentic, and transparent online about the organization they love.

Which approach you take will depend upon the organization, your culture, leadership style, the employee, and their responsibilities. There is not one simple answer. Still, if you keep these guidelines in mind, you will no doubt pick the best approach for each role in your organization.

Roles

Social media changes the responsibilities of traditional corporate roles and requires the creation of entirely new jobs. Below are the most obvious changes to traditional jobs and some of the key new positions created. Use these examples as guidance when planning for the future structure of your organization.

Old Roles, New Responsibilities

These traditional jobs require new responsibilities in the social media world. You should evaluate what these team members have done in the past against what their role should be today and in the future.

Marketing: From Push to Pull

Before social media, traditional marketing roles emphasized push responsibilities. Most marketers focused on advertising, promotions, and creating awareness through disruption of unrelated content. Examples included television commercials breaking up your favorite show, radio commercials while you waited to hear your favorite song, and print ads between your favorite articles. With the emergence of social media technologies, this responsibility shifted from mostly push to mostly pull (inbound) marketing.

In other words, you catch more flies with honey than with vinegar. The old world used vinegar. While people watched their television shows, happily enjoying an episode of the latest drama, they were suddenly disrupted with vinegar. As the show hit a cliffhanger moment, they were left waiting while the network broadcast an ad for the latest cleaning product. Result? Frustrated consumer.

Now, marketing professionals need to use more honey. Instead of using disruptive advertising, which is largely ignored, they need to provide valuable content that consumers seek. If you sell cleaning products, produce a free guide on stain removal. Include valuable advice and coupons to your product. Result? Happy consumer.

Public Relations: From Faux to Frank

In the old world, Public Relations served to present the best image of the organization to the public. With social media, there is greater transparency. Corporate walls guarding culture are now windows. As a result, Public Relations departments now focus more on a frank dialogue about the reality of a given situation. Instead of presenting a veneer identity, a Public Relations department ensures that a candid and balanced story is presented to the public.

It used to be that websites and job descriptions explained entirely the ideal of the organization and none of the reality. Today, that language has softened. Instead of broadly proclaiming, "we are a diverse organization," companies highlight, "we value diversity."

It's not about focusing on every problem within the organization. Instead, your Public Relations department simply needs to be realistic and transparent. Disgruntled employees will speak out in public places. If you have a majority of employees who are happy, you're in good shape, as they will likely defend you. If your culture stinks, you'd better get to work.

Quality Assurance: From Par to Peak

Most companies considered Quality Assurance's role to be achievement of "acceptable" quality levels. Organizations sought to minimize failures rather than excel in quality. Through social media channels, consumers easily identify the product and services with the highest overall quality. Therefore, Quality Assurance now seeks less to achieve par performance and seeks more to achieve peak performance over competition. Consider this scenario:

Old World

A consumer purchases a new electronic device. That device breaks three days after the warranty expires. In the old world, before social media, that consumer would call and complain about the product to the help desk. This incident was then handled individually. In this case, let's say the consumer was offered a replacement product at twenty-five percent off. The consumer is unhappy, but accepts the offer and goes away. The entire interaction took place between one consumer and one help desk person. There was no social media and no public forum, where this frustration could be easily shared. As a result, the quality of your products could remain relatively the same, and few people knew any better or worse.

New World

Today, that same consumer has the problem three days after their warranty is up. Instead of calling your help desk, the most popular option is now to search online for other people with the same problem. As a result, the consumer discovers a large number of people with the same problem. He joins their community. The frustrated group knows you're offering a discount, but remains unimpressed by your quality. Instead, someone mentions that there's a competitor product for about the same price. The competition's product is not experiencing the same failures three days past warranty. So the group buys the competitor product and your sales decline. At the same time, the community provides negative feedback on retail sites about your product. Therefore, your public product reviews rapidly deteriorate. The net result is a quick decline in market share.

In the old world, communication could be contained, whereas the new, more social world is far more open. As a result, maintaining the status quo of your quality assurance could cost your organization.

> *In the old world, communication could be contained, whereas the new, more social world is far more open.*

Customer Service: From Fact to Feel

In the past, Customer Service was positioned by many companies to control post-sale costs rather than to serve the customer. Now that bad customer experiences are quickly shared and escalated to massive scales, it is more important than ever to empathize with unhappy consumers. The best Customer Service departments act more like a consumer advocate and less like a corporate drone.

Corporate drones of the past answered the phone only after a very long hold time. The representatives used a monotone voice and flatly stated the available options to the consumer. If the customer wasn't happy with the result, the answer was often, "I'm sorry sir, but that is our *policy*."

The winning Customer Service departments today answer quickly and in a cheerful voice. They sound surprised to hear of an issue or mention their disappointment at learning of the consumer's trouble. There is positive emotion from the representative. The call usually ends with a satisfied consumer or an attempt to satisfy the consumer through some other means—perhaps a discount on their next purchase?

Human Resources: From Policy to People

At one time, Human Resources existed to protect the company. Human Resources managed people and controlled incidents. Human Resources fought to keep problems quiet and protect corporate reputation, while minimizing lawsuits and overhead costs.

Today, Human Resources finds itself advocating for the engagement, support, and advancement of employees. If Human Resources is not trusted, there's nowhere for disgruntled employees to turn. The result? Unhappy employees turn to venting online, damaging the corporate reputation, and making it more difficult to attract great talent. It's no longer about Human Resources, but about Employee Support.

Employee Support advocates the needs of the teams. This new approach emphasizes transparency over control. The Employee Support objective places less emphasis on short-term cost control and more on long-term benefit maximization.

Celebrity Spokesperson: From Distinction to Dedication

There was a time when a celebrity would do as a spokesperson—any celebrity. Oh sure, it helped if the supermodel touting the features of a minivan was also a mom. But now, not many people believe that same supermodel mom is actually driving the neighborhood kids to the soccer game. As a result, distinction matters less than the celebrity's dedication to the product or service that they sell.

My favorite example is a car commercial featuring the seven-foot-tall, three-hundred-twenty-pound Shaquille O'Neal

(Shaq) driving the too-small Buick LaCrosse. In the commercial, the man can barely fit into half of the car, let alone the driver's seat. Come on . . .

Other examples of disconnected spokespeople can be seen in racing stars. If the celebrity switches out the gear they wore for the race for something new for the post-race interview, just to flash the brand, people notice. Or how about in golf? We care whether the golf star is a family man when the brands that he represents are family brands. If the spokesperson promotes Disney, but is discovered to have a terrible trail of adultery, it matters to those who appreciate family values.

> *The Employee Support objective places less emphasis on short-term cost control and more on long-term benefit maximization.*

In the new world, not just any celebrity will do. If we see somebody touting a product purely for the money, we feel cheap when we wear it. You've bought us. No more. We want quality that a celebrity really uses—not just pretends to use. We want products your endorser is actually dedicated to using.

New Roles

These roles did not exist before social media, but are increasingly important in the social media generation. If you do not have these roles in your organization, you should either create them or address which existing roles own their responsibilities.

Community Manager

The objective of the community manager is to ensure that the quality, value, and, often, growth of a social community remain on track. This work is done by engaging community stakeholders, asking questions, providing content, and bolstering activity in general.

These roles usually report into a marketing or customer service area, and responsibilities vary from company to company and platform to platform. However, one thing is clear: organizations with a large social media presence need community managers.

Community managers today are needed in part because of the rapid growth of social media and diversification of platforms. The role is similar to what brand managers or product champions did in the past. The problem is that many organizations simply are not scaled to handle the massive risk and opportunity of so many platforms.

In the future, this role may merge back into organizations, as the expectations of all employees to engage online becomes paramount. But until you have a culture that advocates and supports such organization-wide engagement, you may need dedicated personnel.

Personas

Businesses don't buy from businesses; people buy from people. As a result, the opportunity for consumers to now have a direct, ongoing discussion with an individual who personifies your brand is outstanding. Dana White of the Ultimate Fighting Championship, whom we discussed earlier, is an excellent example of how stakeholders value connecting with the personification of their favorite brand.

Where the celebrity spokesperson says, "I'm famous and I like this brand," the Persona says, "I am a personification of this brand." The difference is important to understand. Where the spokesperson is an *association with* the brand, the persona is a *representation of* the brand.

The celebrity spokesperson is obviously a paid endorsement and therefore is best seen as an engine for creating awareness and little more. In contrast, the persona is more authentic and not influenced by endorsement money. This authenticity creates a stronger bond and engagement with your stakeholders.

> *Businesses don't buy from businesses; people buy from people.*

When a spokesperson's image no longer aligns with the brands they represent, the brand quickly severs the relationship. With a persona, it is often more difficult, particularly if the persona is an executive in the organization. Therefore, ensuring that your persona's personal and professional values align with your brand is vital.

The persona concept is only partially new. After all, strong personas like Steve Jobs and Bill Gates universally reflected the nature and culture of their organizations long before social media. However, with the evolution of communication technologies, it's now easier than ever for consumers to find personas of your brand—good or bad.

The organization that wants to be proactive about their persona should identify the best person for the role. It need not be the CEO. This could be anyone in the organization—though the more senior, the quicker stakeholders will associate that person as your persona.

Whether it is a role as old as the industry in which you operate or an entirely new role, the principles and values should be consistent. Much like your own leadership, look to the foundation. However, you still need to empower and equip your team with the evolving responsibilities you need to win in this new generation.

Whatever roles you have, you need to provide them with the tools to succeed. One key tool all these parties may need at some point is a Communication Station.

Communication Station

To ensure the greatest effectiveness of their people, larger organizations establish communication stations. These vary in names. In earlier days, those focused solely on social media were often referred to as "Monitoring Stations" or "*Social Media* Monitoring Stations." However, the more evolved stations realize it's not just about social media or monitoring for trouble.

A communication station is a meeting place for cross-functional roles to monitor, share, and manage key messages. For example, you may want employees from the Human Resources, Marketing, and Legal departments addressing something an employee did in public on company time.

These stations typically include several large screens that project real-time posts of relevant content online. You may also project analytics, such as number of people talking about your brand or organization and stakeholders. This way, when something urgent breaks out, such as a major celebrity praising your product, you have immediate awareness and attention. Then, with the right people in the room (from Marketing, Customer Service, and Public Relations), the team can coordinate and build upon the publicity.

Some companies go part-way by seating similar departments, such as Marketing and Public Relations in close proximity.

However, a more comprehensive communication station with well-defined roles, presentation equipment, and guidelines is suggested. Keep in mind that the size of your organization does not preclude you from this. In each aspect of the communication station below, I address suggestions for both large and smaller organizations.

Permanent or Temporary
Larger organizations typically set up a permanent location for these rooms. Smaller organizations are likely to set expectations that, in times of peak demand, a specific conference room or space will be allocated for this purpose.

Location
For the physical structure, consider the message you want to send. Are you seeking to be more open and promote awareness throughout the company? If so, consider high-traffic locations, like near a major entrance, cafeteria, or other gathering space. Do you work in a highly regulated or secretive industry? Perhaps the space needs to be tucked away, where there is less traffic.

Other structure considerations include relevance to executives. Some companies place the station near senior leadership, while others have placed flat screen monitors with specific dashboards and tracking tools near executive offices, with the main room elsewhere.

Layout
Next, consider the layout of the space. If you focus on openness and sharing, you probably want a very open space (or glass walls) and a central pillar where monitors stand for anyone in the space to see.

Whatever the case, consider at least one screen that is not prominently displayed. This is especially important for highly regulated industries that must control their information closely, like financial and medical fields. For smaller organizations that are not investing in a separate space for this room, take these matters into consideration when selecting the temporary meeting room.

Team

Large organizations worry about staffing their communication station 24/7. Smaller teams will need to ensure it's clear to stakeholders when the communication leads are online. That said, it is increasingly difficult to operate an organization and *not* be 24/7. Therefore, consider how you will divide up people. Is it by shifts, role, or another means?

Functions represented should also be considered. Most likely you will want your Public Relations, Marketing, and Customer Service teams represented in the room. Other functions you may want space for include Legal, Sales, and maybe even Research and Development. Whether each function sits in the space full-time or only as needed will be determined by your specific requirements.

Tools

From the time I finish writing this book to the day it hits the shelf, the leading tool solutions have likely changed. So, instead of considering specific names, here are the attributes you want to consider:

- **Remote Access**: Can you access the tool on your mobile device, from any location?
- **Shared Access**: Can multiple individuals and teams access the system with different levels of authorization?
- **Reporting**: Are the reporting capabilities robust enough already, or do you need separate tooling for this?
- **Cool Factor**: If the tool will be used to display streams of content and measurements on large screens, there

is a "cool factor" to be considered. After all, you want your teams to be excited to see and use the tool.

- **Real-Time**: Many media tools are not real-time data, but nightly feeds. This may suffice, but you will definitely want at least one real-time feed solution.

These aspects are important to consider whether you work for a large or small organization. If you are working with a smaller budget though, maximize the functional benefits (access types and real-time) rather than the form or design (reporting and cool factor).

Now that you have the physical space identified and set up, it's time to start using your communication station. In general, there are two types of monitoring activities to get you started: Reactive and Proactive. All organizations should have capabilities in both reactive and proactive monitoring.

Reactive Monitoring

Reactive monitoring is about mitigating trouble. When customers complain publicly, you intercede and take the conversation offline. You want to keep the negative sentiment about your product, service, or brand to a minimum. This type of monitoring and risk mitigation is a fundamental requirement of doing business today. If you're not doing this yet, you should be. This is the starting point of all social media monitoring.

Reactive Monitoring Example

Your new communication station is up and running. You have a small team watching all the social media platforms and public relations outlets for keywords. Suddenly, a member of the monitoring team sends a chat message to the group: "Consumer claims our product burned down their garage." She follows the chat message with a hyperlink. Within minutes, members from Public Relations, Marketing, and Legal have read the consumer's post. Legal is on the phone with product engineering to research the possibility of truth. The entire team gathers in the center meeting space to discuss next steps.

It is quickly decided that the brand's account on that platform should respond saying we are aware of the claim and investigating the matter. Immediately afterward, that same account should contact the consumer and ask them to contact our Customer Service department (who has been notified to expect a call).

As time progresses, the matter can be resolved by the same individuals. The key benefit of this communication station, though, is the monitoring and initial response. Without this co-located group, identification of the issue and response could have easily taken hours. Remember what happened to Kenneth Cole in a matter of hours, as we discussed earlier?

Proactive Monitoring

Proactive monitoring is about capturing the positive sentiment and spreading the love. Many organizations are still not doing this, but it will soon be a fundamental requirement as well. After all, if you're not doing this and your competition is, there is likely a lot more positive sentiment out there for the competition.

Proactive Monitoring Example

Back in your new communication station, the team is hard at work monitoring the media outlets. At one point, one of your community managers stands up and says, in a raised voice, "Wow! Oprah Winfrey just praised our product on her top show during prime time."

The whole team knows what this means—great news. Your organization is about to see a huge spike in sales. In fact, the news is almost too good. You now worry if your production lines can support the sales you now anticipate. So you quickly appoint a lead to follow up with production and ensure they're ready for the demand.

With the production concern being worked, your mind shifts to how you can maximize this opportunity. You pull in the Public Relations and Marketing leads to brainstorm ideas. Within a few minutes, each of their teams is off contacting other influencers, spokespersons, and fans to spread awareness of Oprah's positive review. At the same time, a team has been assembled to update product packaging and promotional material to capture Oprah's comments.

Whether it is reactive or proactive monitoring, you can see how the awareness and response rates enabled by a communication station can help you lead your organization. By focusing on both reactive and proactive monitoring, you can mitigate the negative and escalate the positive.

Whether or not you set up a permanent space consisting of a cross-functional team that is proactively monitoring for good news and bad, you need to be prepared. Have your space identified and ready, then create a social media playbook.

Social Media Playbook

Your social media playbook is an overview of your engagement online. You may find many other components in your own playbook, but this typically includes six major components: Who, What, Where, When, How, and a Crisis Response Plan.

Who and What

Which team members, from which teams, have accountability for what channels? This may be broken down further: for example, Marketing on a particular platform versus Customer Service on the same platform. The plan should name individuals, their contact information, and backups. Make sure this section is updated regularly as employees come and go.

Where

At the most tactical level, what accounts and sites do you manage? This is also a good place to keep record of who has the specific account IDs and passwords. In fact, there should be a master record of every account and password with a trusted few individuals. This way, if the specific contact accountable for a platform is not available in a crisis, the account can still be accessed.

When

This is essentially your hours of operation in each space. As I mentioned earlier, it's harder and harder to work in anything less than 24/7. Still, you may limit around the clock operation to one or two channels. Furthermore, who gets called in when a specific incident occurs should be decided upon. If your organization does not have the resources to operate at all hours, document what hours you are available on each social media platform.

How

This may be governed by your communications policies, or it may be more detailed. Some companies include an explanation of the tone of voice they want employees to use. For example, maybe you want employees to come across as funny, quirky, or serious. This is guided by the brand and image. That said, showing concern for the stakeholder is never a bad idea.

Crisis Response Plan

Arguably the most important component, and possibly independent of the playbook, your crisis plan is the step-by-step guide to handling a crisis when it occurs. Who gets called under what conditions? When is legal action required? When should an executive be notified? These are all questions answered in your crisis plan.

To make your crisis plan most effective, you should do crisis response drills. Like fire drills, you run the team through the steps of a crisis response as though one were occurring. There are companies that do this as part of their engagement. They will walk your employee teams through a series of events that they must respond to and provide feedback at the conclusion of the drill.

Your playbook is all about preparation and expectations. Without a playbook such as this, you may be perfectly fine. However, you could also experience a disaster. The latter can be mitigated, if not avoided entirely, with a playbook. The question is whether you will be prepared when that disaster occurs.

Of course, the best defense is a strong offense. In social media, a strong offense means putting your best players—or even the full team—on the field. That team is your social media army.

Your Social Media Army

Sadly, the phrase "our employees are our greatest assets" has become a cliché. The reality is that many organizations ignore the tremendous potential benefits offered by their employees. Nowhere is the complete ignorance of this opportunity more obvious than in the lack of effective utilization of employees in social media.

As social media communications evolved, companies began blocking employee access to the sites. In so doing, these companies not only prevented employees from using social media at work, they also told their employees they couldn't be trusted—especially in social media. The net result was not only preventing access, but also suggesting that business and social media were never to merge.

Later, as companies began to see some business benefits of the tools, many leaders begrudgingly relented, insisting on close monitoring of employee activity on these platforms. Still, few leaders realize the social media army they are keeping locked up. Your greatest asset—your people—may be sitting on the shelf, collecting dust. Instead of leaving this asset collecting dust, why not empower and engage it in your business?

Your greatest asset—your people—may be sitting on the shelf, collecting dust.

Awareness
Increase the social media awareness of your employees by placing monitors of relevant discussions for your mission, industry, and people in hallways. Show your people where competitors are engaging online and where you are doing a good or bad job. Produce a regular directory of social media accounts held by the company. Better yet, let employees share their personal accounts internally so they can find each other and engage on platforms together.

Training
Train your people on how to respond online. Provide the risks and examples they can see. For example, how did someone in your industry do a good job handling a customer complaint online? How should employees respond to similar complaints?

Use the principles in this book, or develop your own. Share them with employees as a guide for their engagement when discussing business. Repeat the corporate values and brand messaging your employees should already know. Those same values and brand messaging will work online.

Certification

Why not certify employees as advocates in social media? There's no public standard for such certification but you can create one specific to your organization. Employees can still be expected to state that the opinion is their own and not official business, but they can be encouraged to advocate for the company online.

There could even be levels of certification. The first level would be basic certification, required of all employees. Then, you could have a more advanced certification for your "brand advocates." Individuals with the more advanced training may be listed on the company website as employees who could be found in social channels.

Sharing links to employee social media accounts boosts the employee's profile. This both increases their social proof and reminds them of their responsibility to be an advocate and positive influence for your mission in social channels.

Mobilization

This army may not be effective at protecting the organization at all times. However, when a crisis hits and you really need that army, you can mobilize the team to counter negative communications with positive advocacy—transparently. Again, all employees should disclose their relationship. However, the positive sentiment from many employees will still be social proof—especially if their connections join the positive sentiment bandwagon.

One great example of this is GoDaddy.com.[74] There is plenty of negative sentiment about GoDaddy's hosting and related services. However, when a major incident seems to break, there is a flood of positive sentiment along with it. This is often initiated by GoDaddy employees offering items like discounts, promotions, or other positive-sentiment driving information. As a result, the overall sentiment about GoDaddy.com remains fairly neutral.

If you ever feel like your social media presence is lacking, ask yourself, "Where is the army?" Are you leaving your greatest asset to waste away on the shelf? If so, engage and mobilize your social media army.

There are many matters to address when rolling out social media engagement across your organization. In addition to your own leadership by example, the tools, techniques and processes we covered here may help your organization establish a firm foundation.

Your Organization Summary

To be effective at driving social media benefits across your organization, a leader should:

1. Understand that engaging the organization in social media requires effective management through all the stages of change.
2. Prepare effective policies and procedures for the organization as guidelines.
3. Understand and implement the shifting responsibilities for employees as well as new roles.
4. Create a communication station or have a plan to execute one when needed.
5. Build and rehearse a social media playbook.
6. Mobilize their greatest asset as a social media army.

Reflection

1. Where should you place your communications station, and who should be in it?
2. Are your existing policies and procedures adequate to cover social media demands?
3. How have the roles and responsibilities of your team changed in the post social media revolution world?

CLOSING

Leadership is not easy, but you have tools that make it easier now than in any previous generation. With the proper understanding and use of these tools, you can strengthen your leadership and the success of your mission.

The principles of great leadership have not changed throughout history. However, how you practice those principles must evolve with the technology and expectations of the present.

As a leader, you can be most effective by understanding how social media and leadership dovetail with how you Lead People, Your Platform, Your Principles, and Your Organization. A quick review of these concepts follows.

Leading People

Leadership is personal again. The leader needs to understand this concept by reflecting trust and personal engagement. There are many kinds of trust, all of which, when practiced, decrease costs and increase speed. In social media, trust is critical for speed and success.

We are in a new era of communication, the era of Mass Dialogue. In the past, conversation was largely one-way on a massive scale. Today, a leader may not be able to hold a million conversations; however, he or she can have conversations with single individuals that represent thousands of like-minded people, and those conversations are held in front of millions.

Corporate and leadership veneers are dead. In the past, leaders and organizations could pretend to be one thing to the external world and act entirely different inside the office walls. Social media turned those brick walls into glass. There's no longer anywhere to hide. If you've got a bad culture, it will hurt you. If you have a great culture, you've got a jumpstart on the competition.

Your Platform

Anyone can organize and lead the message or mission. To organize your stakeholders, build a platform and be a passionate content publisher.

There are three online platform models for leaders: Stronghold, Spider Web, and Hub and Spoke. Many leaders begin with a stronghold or spider web model. That's fine, but you should evolve into a hub and spoke model for maximum reach and minimum maintenance effort.

Your platform offers many benefits. Among these benefits are:

- **Leverage**: The ability to rely on your network for support
- **Reach**: The ability to align constituents within and beyond your platform
- **Global**: The ability to extend your message around the world
- **Conversion**: The ability to understand what message drives the best results

Every leader makes mistakes. The employees of your organization make mistakes too. When those mistakes happen, you will want your social media platform in place to extend your influence. Establishing one after a mistake occurs is too late.

Your Principles

The key principles for Social Leadership are present in the acronym S-O-C-I-A-L. For each principle, we saw examples of success and failure. These examples were timeless, represented by leaders from the American Revolution, and time*ly*, as represented by contemporary leaders. Because Listening comes first and Service is the cornerstone, we covered these principles in reverse order:

Listen

You must listen to your stakeholders or suffer the consequences of a disconnected leader. Listen to your stakeholders before you engage in new communities, or you may engage in an offensive manner. There are three categories of listening to embrace: comprehensive, real-time, and analytical listening.

Action-Oriented

Responsiveness and timeliness affect results more today than ever. A moment in social media can impact an eternity of results. To ensure responding in the timeliest manner, provide training for your team, create template messages, and employ monitoring solutions.

Integrity
Your stakeholders see through smoke and mirrors with x-ray vision in social media. Ensure that your values—both on and off the clock—align with the values of your organization. To reinforce this concept, make the time and effort to document your own values. Then ensure that values-based hiring is emphasized across the organization.

Connect
Understand your network and those of your stakeholders. Respect the power behind the connections of others. When hiring and recruiting stakeholders, consider the connections they have and the overlap with those already in the organization. Remember, it's not just about the quantity of connections, but the quality and level of engagement as well.

Open
Your stakeholders can only support you if they know your honest intentions. If you mask reality, it may help in the short-term but kill you in the long-term. Worse, collateral damage could hit your stakeholders hard. To be open with your stakeholders, be aware of the risks inherent at times of weakness and ask yourself some key questions before sharing content on social media.

Serve
Service is the core of great leadership. Great leadership is Servant Leadership. With the growth of social media, the demand for Servant Leadership is greater than ever before. Servant Leadership is being Selfless, Empathetic, Resolute, Virtuous, Authentic, Nascent, and Thorough (S-E-R-V-A-N-T).

Leadership beyond the social media revolution is about maximizing the timeless principles of great leadership in contemporary environments. We do this by following those principles above, with Servant Leadership at the root of all we do, both online and off.

Your Organization

As a leader, you need to structure your organization to best leverage the leadership opportunities afforded you through social media. This won't happen overnight. There are several stages of change that you must work through.

There is a right way and a wrong way to handle the policies and procedures for communication in this mass dialogue era. It is important to emphasize enablement and empowerment of your team with only the absolutely necessary amount of oversight and control.

The responsibilities and expectations of roles in the new world are changing. Marketing has evolved from push to pull; Public Relations from faux to frank; Quality Assurance from par to peak; Customer Service from fact to feel; and Human Resources from policy to people. There are also new roles to create: Community Managers and Personas.

As you evolve your teams, you also need to adjust the spaces in which they work. In particular, you'll want to create, or at least plan for, a communication station. In addition, make sure you keep the Social Media playbook—or, minimally, a crisis response plan—in that station and available to your team. Most important of all, remember your people truly are your greatest asset. Then treat them as such.

Be a Better Leader

Through your People, Platform, Principles, and Organization, you can strengthen your influence, improve your leadership, and better serve stakeholders. The question is simply this: will you take the principles of great leadership and apply them as effectively as possible in this new world? Will you be a revolutionary leader who flips your paradigm, or will you instead pursue the practices of the old empirical leaders?

Revolutionary or Empirical Leader?

During the American Revolution, the American colonist leaders were great at leveraging old world social media to their benefit. These leaders practiced the principles listed here effectively. They Served their stakeholders, were Open about their intentions, Connected across many networks, served with Integrity, were Action-Oriented, and Listened to the concerns of their people. In contrast, their British leadership counterparts failed to practice these social media principles consistently.

The technology of colonial America limited the social media capacity and ability of leaders. Today, social media technology enables, empowers, and demands greater leadership. Therefore, you can choose to join the revolution that champions this technology and lead a successful campaign, or the alternative is clear.

Which side are you on in the social media revolution? Do your stakeholders associate you with the practices of colonial American patriots or those of the old British Empire?

I encourage you to join the revolution . . . Yorktown is near, and the French are approaching. On which side of the battle lines does your leadership reside?

EPILOGUE

The U.S. Presidential Election from the introduction is long over. The horrible sentiment created in social waves about Katy's Home Appliances has settled to a low ripple, following the Obama's Dead Grandmother incident. In fact, overall sentiment for that brand online is almost back to normal levels.

The return of Katy's Home Appliances to normal sentiment was no accident. It occurred through the decisive action of brand leaders to respond using many of the principles in this book. As a result, the community appreciated their authentic response and responded, more or less, in kind.

More importantly, Katy's Home Appliances did not stop there. In several follow-up conversations with the Marketing and Public Relations leadership, it was clear that they planned to better prepare leaders for influence in the social media revolution.

I hope you never have to manage a social media crisis like the one that October evening. Whether or not you face such a crisis, practicing the principles in this book will extend your influence and help you to better serve stakeholders with greater leadership. Here's to leading with a flipped paradigm!

Thank You

Thank you for reading *Paradigm Flip*. I am truly honored that you committed this time and effort to digesting my advice. I hope you found this beneficial to the growth of your leadership and the success of your mission. If you have any thoughts on this topic, I'd love to get your feedback. You can reach me anytime at ModernServantLeader.com.

Thank you and remember: keep serving.

NOTES

[1] This incident is a true story, but I've changed the brand name to assuage the company.

[2] "Fad," Urban Dictionary, last modified February 31, 2003, accessed July 5, 2013, http://www.urbandictionary.com/define.php?term=fad.

[3] Jim Edwards, "BRUTAL: 50% Decline In TV Viewership Shows Why Your

[2] "Fad," Urban Dictionary, last modified February 31, 2003, accessed July 5, 2013, http://www.urbandictionary.com/define.php?term=fad.

[3] Jim Edwards, "BRUTAL: 50% Decline In TV Viewership Shows Why Your Cable Bill Is So High," Yahoo! Finance, published January 31, 2013, accessed July 5, 2013, http://finance.yahoo.com/news/brutal-50-decline-tv-viewership-160856096.html.

[4] Gary Vaynerchuk, "Gary Vaynerchuk - Keynote Speech at Inc 500 Seminar 2011," YouTube, video, 1:01:12, published December 17, 2011, accessed July 5, 2013, http://www.youtube.com/watch?v=IcqCAqZtedI.

[5] Jim Collins, Good to Great: Why Some Companies Make the Leap . . . and Others Don't (New York: HarperBusiness, 2001).

[6] Facebook, accessed June 6, 2013, https://www.facebook.com/.

[7] Wikipedia, accessed June 6, 2013, http://www.wikipedia.org/.

[8] Nielsen. "Trust in Advertising and Brand Messages. April 2012. Web. June 21, 2013.
http://nielsen.com/content/dam/corporate/ie/newsletters/Ireland%20Trust%20in%20Ad%20article%202012.pdf

[9] Gary Vaynerchuk, Crush It!: Why NOW Is the Time to Cash In on Your Passion (New York: HarperCollins, 2009).

[10] Jim Lecinski, Winning the Zero Moment of Truth—ZMOT (Vook, 2011), Kindle edition.

[11] Toby Ward, "Beehive builds buzz at IBM," Prescient Digital Media, accessed June 5, 2013, http://www.prescientdigital.com/articles/intranet-articles/beehive-builds-buzz-at-ibm/.

[12] McGonigal, Jane. "Reality Is Broken: Why Games Make Us Better and How They Can Change the World". Penguin Books. December 27, 2011.

[13] Outliers: The Story of Success, Malcom Gladwell, Black Bay Books, November 2008.

[14] "Arab Spring." Wikipedia, The Free Encyclopedia. Wikimedia Foundation, Inc. 4 June, 2013. Web. 5 June, 2013.
http://en.wikipedia.org/wiki/Arab_Spring .

[15] Michael Hyatt, Platform: Get Noticed in a Noisy World (Nashville: Thomas Nelson Publishers, 2012)

[16] Renegades Write the Rules: How the Digital Royalty Use Social Media to Innovate, Amy Jo Martin, Jossey-Bass, October 2, 2012.

[17] Glassdoor. Glassdoor. "Best Places to Work." 13 November, 2012. Web. 5 June, 2013. http://www.glassdoor.com/Best-Places-to-Work-LST_KQ0,19.htm .

[18] eMarketer. eMarketer. "CEOs Who Tweet Held in High Regard." 27 March 2012. Web. 5 June, 2013. http://www.emarketer.com/Article/CEOs-Who-Tweet-Held-High-Regard/1008929

[19] The SPEED of Trust: The One Thing that Changes Everything, October 17, 2006, Stephen M. R. Covey

[20] "Behind the Enron Scandal," Time Lists, accessed June 5, 2013, http://www.time.com/time/specials/packages/0,28757,2021097,00.html

[21] Chris Brogan and Julien Smith. Trust Agents Using the Web to Build Influence, Improve Reputation, and Earn Trust (Hoboken: John Wiley & Sons, 2010).

[22] Marshall Kirkpatrick, "Google CEO Schmidt: 'People Aren't Ready for the Technology Revolution,'" ReadWrite, published August 4, 2010, accessed June 5, 2013,

http://readwrite.com/2010/08/04/google_ceo_schmidt_people_arent_rea
dy_for_the_tech

[23] Secret of My Success, directed by Herbert Ross (Universal Pictures, 1987), DVD.

[24] "Conversion," Dictionary.com, Random House Inc., accessed June 5, 2013, http://dictionary.reference.com/browse/conversion.

[25] Indiana Jones and the Last Crusade, directed by Steven Spielberg (Paramount Pictures, 1989), DVD.

[26] "Giveaway: Intimate Dinner for Two at Sotto Terra," Seriously Soupy, published August 18, 2011, accessed July 5, 2013, http://seriouslysoupy.com/giveaway-intimate-dinner-for-two-at-sotto-terra/.

[27] Andrew Adam Newman, "Bloggers Don't Follow the Script to ConAgra's Chagrin," The New York Times, published September 6, 2011, accessed June 5, 2013, http://www.nytimes.com/2011/09/07/business/media/when-bloggers-dont-follow-the-script-to-conagras-chagrin.html?pagewanted=all

[28] "Conagra Ketchum and food bloggers," Google, accessed June 5, 2013, https://www.google.com/search?q=Conagra+Ketchum+and+food+bloggers&sugexp=chrome,mod=15&sourceid=chrome&ie=UTF-8

[29] Follower ratio is the number of Followers to the Number of people you follow. A higher follower ratio suggests a greater quality of followers. Follower Ratio = Following : Followers.

[30] At the time of first publication, Google Alerts is the most popular: "Google Alerts," Google, accessed June 5, 2013, http://www.google.com/alerts.

[31] At the time of first publication, my preference is for Hootsuite (HootSuite, accessed July 7, 2013, https://hootsuite.com/) or Tweetdeck ("Tweetdeck by Twitter," Twitter, accessed July 7, 2013, http://tweetdeck.com/).

[32] Nick Beske, "Travelling at the Speed of Social Media," PointClick Productions, published April 11, 2012, accessed June 5, 2013, http://www.pointclickproductions.com/blog/traveling-at-the-speed-of-social-media.

[33] Dominique Wilson, "Newark Mayor Cory Booker," YouTube, video, 0:30, published December 28, 2010, accessed June 5, 2013, http://www.youtube.com/watch?v=nqzhIX-mb5M.

[34] "Cory Booker Twitter Blizzard," Google, accessed June 5, 2013, https://www.google.com/search?q=Cory+Booker+Twitter+Blizzard&aq=f&sugexp=chrome, mod=5&sourceid=chrome&ie=UTF-8.

[35] Mary Phillips-Sandy, "Kenneth Cole's Egypt Tweet Offends Just About Everyone on Twitter," *AOL News*, published February 3, 2011, accessed June 5, 2013c http://www.aolnews.com/2011/02/03/kenneth-coles-egypt-tweet-offends-just-about-everyone-on-twitte/.

[36] "KENNETH COLE, MEET @KENNETHCOLEPR," *Life, In Digital* (blog), published February 3, 2011, accessed June 5, 2013, http://lizzjudd.wordpress.com/2011/02/03/kennethcole-vs-kennethcolepr/.

[37] @fakeKennethCole, "Fake Kenneth Cole," *Twitter*, accessed June 5, 2013, https://twitter.com/fakekennethcole.

[38] "'Kenneth Cole' Cairo," *Google*, accessed June 5, 2013, https://www.google.com/#hl=en&q=%22Kenneth+Cole%22+Cairo.

[39] Tom Kelley. "How Important is Culture to the Success of Your Organization?" *Portland Human Resource Management Association* (blog), published November 3, 2012, accessed June 6, 2013, www.portlandhrmablog.org/?p=637.

[40] Charles A. Grymes, "The Militia," *Virginia Places*, accessed June 6, 2013, http://www.virginiaplaces.org/military/revwarfought.html.

[41] *The Patriot*, directed by Roland Emmerich (Columbia Pictures, 2000), Blu-ray.

[42] Michael Hyatt. *Michael Hyatt: Intentional Leadership*, accessed July 10, 2013, http://michaelhyatt.com/.

[43] Generally Accepted Accounting Principles—the legal terms by which public corporations are expected to file financial reports.

[44] Malcom Gladwell, *The Tipping Point: How Little Things Can Make a Big Difference* (Back Bay Books, 2002).

[45] Chris Brogan and Julien Smith. *Trust Agents Using the Web to Build Influence, Improve Reputation, and Earn Trust* (Hoboken: John Wiley & Sons, 2010).

[46] Jose Antonio Vargas, "Obama Raised Half a Billion Online," *The Washington Post*, published November 20, 2008, accessed June 6, 2013, http://voices.washingtonpost.com/44/2008/11/20/obama_raised_half_a_billion_on.html.

[47] Daniel Nations, "How Barack Obama is Using Web 2.0 to Run for President," *Computing Web Trends*, About.com, accessed June 6, 2013, http://webtrends.about.com/od/web20/a/obama-web.htm.

[48] Ellen McGirt, "How Chris Hughes Helped Launch Facebook and the Barack Obama Campaign," *Fast Company*, published April 1, 2009, accessed July 10, 2013, http://www.fastcompany.com/1207594/how-chris-hughes-helped-launch-facebook-and-barack-obama-campaign.

[49] "The Social Pulpit: Barack Obama's Social Media Toolkit," Edelman, published 2009, accessed June 6, 2013, http://blog.guykawasaki.com/OBAMA%20SNA%20Strategic_1.pdf.

[50] I confess, I neither know, nor care which sister.

[51] Jenny Lawson, "UPDATED: And Then the PR Guy Called Me a 'F*cking B*tch'. I Can't Even Make This Sh*t Up," *The Bloggess*, last modified October 6, 2011, accessed June 6, 2013, http://thebloggess.com/2011/10/and-then-the-pr-guy-called-me-a-fucking-bitch-i-cant-even-make-this-shit-up/.

[52] "BrandLink Communications," *Google*, accessed June 7, 2013, https://www.google.com/search?q=%E2%80%9CBrandLink+Communications%E2%80%9D&oq=%E2%80%9CBrandLink+Communications%E2%80%9D&aqs=chrome.0.57j0l3j62.1083j0&sourceid=chrome&ie=UTF-8.

[53] "LinkedIn Maps," *LinkedIn*, accessed October 12, 2013, http://inmaps.linkedinlabs.com/ sharing encouraged via http://blog.linkedin.com/2011/01/24/linkedin-inmaps/

[54] "John Hancock," Signers of the Declaration of Independence, *USHistory.org*, published July 4, 1995, accessed June 6, 2013, http://www.ushistory.org/declaration/signers/hancock.htm.

[55] Jill LePore, "Was Thomas Paine too much of a freethinker for the country he helped free?" The Sharpened Quill, *The New Yorker*, published October 16, 2006, accessed June 6, 2013, http://www.newyorker.com/archive/2006/10/16/061016crbo_books.

[56] Marg Baskin, "An Answer to That Part of the Narrative of Lieutenant-General Sir Henry Clinton, K.B. which Relates to the Conduct of Lieutenant-General Earl Cornwallis, During the Campaign in North America, in the Year 1781," last modified January 2, 2011, accessed June 6, 2013, http://home.golden.net/~marg/bansite/src/cornwallis0.html.

[57] "Mike Parry, Minnesota State Senate Candidate, Defends Racist Twitter Message," Huff Post Politics, *Huffington Post*, last modified May 25, 2011, accessed June 7, 2013, http://www.huffingtonpost.com/2010/01/06/mike-parry-minnesota-stat_n_413200.html.

[58] Jessica Durando, "BP's Tony Hayward: 'I'd like my life back,'" *USA Today*, published June 1, 2010, accessed June 7, 2013, http://content.usatoday.com/communities/greenhouse/post/2010/06/bp-tony-hayward-apology/1#.UbTo5JWlafQ.

[59] "George Washington's Commission as Commander in Chief," *Library of Congress* (online), published July 30, 2010, accessed July 14, 2013, http://www.loc.gov/rr/program/bib/ourdocs/commission.html.

[60] Mary Stockwell, "Newburgh Address (1783)," *George Washington's Mount Vernon*, accessed July 14, 2013, http://www.mountvernon.org/educational-resources/encyclopedia/newburgh-address.

[61] "George Washington's Resignation," *Maryland State House*, published 2007, accessed July 14, 2013, http://msa.maryland.gov/msa/mdstatehouse/html/gwresignation.html.

[62] Carl G. Karsch, "The First Continental Congress: A Dangerous Journey Begins," Carpenters' Hall, *USHistory*.org, accessed July 14, 2013, http://www.ushistory.org/carpentershall/history/congress.htm.

[63] Tony Hsieh, *Delivering Happiness* (New York: Business Plus, 2010).

[64] Jack Welch and Suzy Welch, "The Case for 20-70-10," *Bloomberg BusinessWeek*, published October 1, 2006, accessed June 6, 2013, http://www.businessweek.com/stories/2006-10-01/the-case-for-20-70-10.

[65] "The Struggle to Measure Performance," *Bloomberg BusinessWeek*, published January 8, 2006, accessed June 6, 2013, http://www.businessweek.com/stories/2006-01-08/the-struggle-to-measure-performance.

[66] Tim Irwin, *Derailed: Five Lessons Learned from Catastrophic Failures of Leadership* (Nashville: Thomas Nelson, 2009).

[67] *Robert K. Greenleaf Center for Servant Leadership*, accessed June 6, 2013, http://www.greenleaf.org/.

[68] Jim Collins, *Good to Great: Why Some Companies Make the Leap... and Others Don't* (New York, NY: Harper-Collins, 2001).

[69] Larry Spears can be reached via *Spears Center for Servant Leadership* at SpearsCenter.org

[70] Robert K. Greenleaf, *The Servant as Leader* (Westfield, IN: The Greenleaf Center for Servant Leadership, 2008).

[71] Larry C. Spears and Michele Lawrence, *Practicing Servant Leadership: Succeeding Through Trust, Bravery, and Forgiveness* (San Francisco: Jossey-Bass, 2004).

[72] Jim Collins, *Good to Great: Why Some Companies Make the Leap... and Others Don't* (New York, NY: Harper-Collins, 2001).

[73] "The Transtheoretical Model of Behavioral Change," *The Habits Lab at UMBC*, accessed June 6, 2013, http://www.umbc.edu/psyc/habits/content/the_model/.

[74] *GoDaddy.com*, accessed June 9, 2013, http://www.godaddy.com/.

Bibliography

@fakeKennethCole. "Fake Kenneth Cole." *Twitter*. Accessed June 5, 2013. https://twitter.com/fakekennethcole.

"Behind the Enron Scandal." *Time Lists*. Accessed June 5, 2013. http://www.time.com/time/specials/packages/0,28757,2021097,00.html.

Beske, Nick. "Travelling at the Speed of Social Media." *PointClick Productions*. Published April 11, 2012. Accessed June 5, 2013. http://www.pointclickproductions.com/blog/traveling-at-the-speed-of-social-media.

"BrandLink Communications." *Google*. Accessed June 7, 2013. https://www.google.com/search?q=%E2%80%9CBrandLink+Communications%E2%80%9D&oq=%E2%80%9CBrandLink+Communications%E2%80%9D&aqs=chrome.0.57j0l3j62.1083j0&sourceid=chrome&ie=UTF-8.

Brogan, Chris, and Julien Smith. *Trust Agents Using the Web to Build Influence, Improve Reputation, and Earn Trust.* Hoboken: John Wiley & Sons, 2010.

Collins, Jim. *Good to Great: Why Some Companies Make the Leap . . . and Others Don't.* New York: HarperBusiness, 2001.

"Conagra Ketchum and Food Blogger." *Google.* Accessed August 5, 2013. https://www.google.com/search?q=Conagra+Ketchum+and+Food+Bloggers&oq=Conagra+Ketchum+and+Food+Bloggers&aqs=chrome.0.69i57j0.752j0&sourceid=chrome&ie=UTF-8#bav=on.2,or.r_cp.r_qf.&cad=b&fp=81bbfe24b99ff94c&q=Conagra+Ketchum+and+Food+Blogger.

"Conversion." *Dictionary.com.* Random House Inc. Accessed June 5, 2013. http://dictionary.reference.com/browse/conversion.

"Cory Booker Twitter Blizzard." *Google.* Accessed June 5, 2013. https://www.google.com/search?q=Cory+Booker+Twitter+Blizzard&aq=f&sugexp=chrome,mod=5&sourceid=chrome&ie=UTF-8.

Durando, Jessica. "BP's Tony Hayward: 'I'd like my life back.'" *USA Today.* Published June 1, 2010. Accessed June 7, 2013. http://content.usatoday.com/communities/greenhouse/post/2010/06/bp-tony-hayward-apology/1#.UbTo5JWlafQ.

Edward, Jim. "BRUTAL: 50% Decline In TV Viewership Shows Why Your Cable Bill Is So High." *Yahoo! Finance.* Last modified January 31, 2013. Accessed July 5, 2013. http://finance.yahoo.com/news/brutal-50-decline-tv-viewership-160856096.html.

Facebook. Accessed June 6, 2013. https://www.facebook.com/.

"Fad." *Urban Dictionary*. Last modified February 31, 2003. Accessed July 5, 2013. http://www.urbandictionary.com/define.php?term=fad.javascript:void(0);

"George Washington's Commission as Commander in Chief." *Library of Congress* (online). Published July 30, 2010. Accessed July 14, 2013. http://www.loc.gov/rr/program/bib/ourdocs/commission.html.

"George Washington's Resignation." *Maryland State House*. Published 2007. Accessed July 14, 2013. http://msa.maryland.gov/msa/mdstatehouse/html/gwresignation.html.

"Giveaway: Intimate Dinner for Two at Sotto Terra." *Seriously Soupy*. Published August 18, 2011. Accessed July 5, 2013. http://seriouslysoupy.com/giveaway-intimate-dinner-for-two-at-sotto-terra/.

Gladwell, Malcom. *The Tipping Point: How Little Things Can Make a Big Difference*. Back Bay Books, 2002. *GoDaddy.com*. Accessed June 9, 2013. http://www.godaddy.com/.javascript:void(0);

"Google Alerts." *Google*. Accessed June 5, 2013. http://www.google.com/alerts.

Greenleaf, Robert K. *The Servant as Leader*. Westfield, IN: The Greenleaf Center for Servant Leadership, 2008.

Grymes, Charles A. "The Militia." *Virginia Places*. Accessed June 6, 2013. http://www.virginiaplaces.org/military/revwarfought.html.

Henriques, Diana B. "Madoff is Sentenced to 150 Years for Ponzi Scheme." *The New York Times*. Published June 29,

2009. Accessed June 5, 2013.
http://www.nytimes.com/2009/06/30/business/30ma
doff.html?ref=bernardlmadoff&_r=0.

Hsieh, Tony. *Delivering Happiness*. New York: Business Plus, 2010.

Hugo, Victor. *The History of a Crime.* New York: Mondial, 2005.

Hyatt, Michael. *Michael Hyatt: Intentional Leadership.* Accessed July 10, 2013. http://michaelhyatt.com/.

Hyatt, Michael. *Platform: Get Noticed in a Noisy World.* Nashville: Thomas Nelson Publishers, 2012.

Indiana Jones and the Last Crusade. Directed by Steven Spielberg. Paramount Pictures, 1989. DVD.

Irwin, Tim. *Derailed: Five Lessons Learned from Catastrophic Failures of Leadership.* Nashville: Thomas Nelson, 2009.

"John Hancock." Signers of the Declaration of Independence. *USHistory.org.* Published July 4, 1995. Accessed June 6, 2013.
http://www.ushistory.org/declaration/signers/hancock
.htm.

Karsch, Carl G. "The First Continental Congress: A Dangerous Journey Begins." Carpenters' Hall. *USHistory.org.* Accessed July 14, 2013.
http://www.ushistory.org/carpentershall/history/cong
ress.htm.

Kelley, Tom. "How Important is Culture to the Success of Your Organization?" *Portland Human Resource Management Association* (blog). Published November 3, 2012. Accessed June 6, 2013.
www.portlandhrmablog.org/?p=637.

"'Kenneth Cole' Cairo." *Google.* Accessed June 5, 2013.
https://www.google.com/#hl=en&q=%22Kenneth+Col
e%22+Cairo.

"KENNETH COLE, MEET @KENNETHCOLEPR." *Life, In Digital* (blog). Published February 3, 2011. Accessed June 5, 2013. http://lizzjudd.wordpress.com/2011/02/03/kennethcole-vs-kennethcolepr/.

Kirkpatrick, Marshall. "Google CEO Schmidt: 'People Aren't Ready for the Technology Revolution.'" *ReadWrite*. Published August 4, 2010. Accessed June 5, 2013. http://readwrite.com/2010/08/04/google_ceo_schmidt_people_arent_ready_for_the_tech.

Kruse, Kevin. "100 Best Quotes on Leadership." *Forbes*. Published October 16, 2012. Accessed August 7, 2013. http://www.forbes.com/sites/kevinkruse/2012/10/16/quotes-on-leadership/.

Lawson, Jenny. "UPDATED: And Then the PR Guy Called Me a 'F*cking B*tch'. I Can't Even Make This Sh*t Up." *The Bloggess*. Last modified October 6, 2011. Accessed June 6, 2013. http://thebloggess.com/2011/10/and-then-the-pr-guy-called-me-a-fucking-bitch-i-cant-even-make-this-shit-up/.

Lecinski, Jim. *Winning the Zero Moment of Truth—ZMOT*. Vook, 2011. Kindle edition.

LePore, Jill. "Was Thomas Paine too much of a freethinker for the country he helped free?" The Sharpened Quill. *The New Yorker*. Published October 16, 2006. Accessed June 6, 2013. http://www.newyorker.com/archive/2006/10/16/061016crbo_books.

"LinkedIn Maps." *LinkedIn*. Accessed June 7, 2013. http://inmaps.linkedinlabs.com/.

McGirt, Ellen. "How Chris Hughes Helped Launch Facebook and the Barack Obama Campaign." *Fast Company*. Published April 1, 2009. Accessed July 10, 2013.

http://www.fastcompany.com/1207594/how-chris-hughes-helped-launch-facebook-and-barack-obama-campaign.

"Mike Parry, Minnesota State Senate Candidate, Defends Racist Twitter Message." Huff Post Politics. *Huffington Post*. Last modified May 25, 2011. Accessed June 7, 2013. http://www.huffingtonpost.com/2010/01/06/mike-parry-minnesota-stat_n_413200.html.

Nations, Daniel. "How Barack Obama is Using Web 2.0 to Run for President." *Computing Web Trends*. About.com. Accessed June 6, 2013. http://webtrends.about.com/od/web20/a/obama-web.htm.

Newman, Andrew Adam. "Bloggers Don't Follow the Script to ConAgra's Chagrin." *The New York Times*. Published September 6, 2011. Accessed June 5, 2013. http://www.nytimes.com/2011/09/07/business/media/when-bloggers-dont-follow-the-script-to-conagras-chagrin.html?pagewanted=all.

Phillips-Sandy, Mary. "Kenneth Cole's Egypt Tweet Offends Just About Everyone on Twitter." *AOL News*. Published February 3, 2011. Accessed June 5, 2013. http://www.aolnews.com/2011/02/03/kenneth-coles-egypt-tweet-offends-just-about-everyone-on-twitte/.

Secret of My Success. Directed by Herbert Ross. Universal Pictures, 1987. DVD.

"Social Media Management." *HootSuite*. Accessed July 7, 2013. https://hootsuite.com/.

Spears, Larry C. and Michele Lawrence. *Practicing Servant Leadership: Succeeding Through Trust, Bravery, and Forgiveness*. San Francisco: Jossey-Bass, 2004.

Spears, Larry. "Spears Center for Servant Leadership." *SpearsCenter.org*. Accessed June 8, 2013. http://www.spearscenter.org/.

Stockwell, Mary. "Newburgh Address (1783)." *George Washington's Mount Vernon*. Accessed July 14, 2013. http://www.mountvernon.org/educational-resources/encyclopedia/newburgh-address.

"The Social Pulpit: Barack Obama's Social Media Toolkit." Edelman. Published 2009. Accessed June 6, 2013. http://blog.guykawasaki.com/OBAMA%20SNA%20Strategic_1.pdf.

"The Struggle to Measure Performance." *Bloomberg BusinessWeek*. Published January 8, 2006. Accessed June 6, 2013. http://www.businessweek.com/stories/2006-01-08/the-struggle-to-measure-performance.

"The Transtheoretical Model of Behavioral Change." *The Habits Lab at UMBC*. Accessed June 6, 2013. http://www.umbc.edu/psyc/habits/content/the_model/.

"Tweetdeck by Twitter." *Twitter*. Accessed July 7, 2013. http://tweetdeck.com/.

Robert K. Greenleaf Center for Servant Leadership. Accessed June 6, 2013. http://www.greenleaf.org/.

Vargas, Jose Antonio. "Obama Raised Half a Billion Online." *The Washington Post*. Published November 20, 2008. Accessed June 6, 2013. http://voices.washingtonpost.com/44/2008/11/20/obama_raised_half_a_billion_on.html.

Vaynerchuk, Gary. *Crush It!: Why NOW Is the Time to Cash In on Your Passion*. New York: HarperCollins, 2009.

Vaynerchuk, Gary. "Gary Vaynerchuk - Keynote Speech at Inc 500 Seminar 2011." *YouTube*. Video, 1:01:12.

Published December 17, 2011. Accessed July 5, 2013.
http://www.youtube.com/watch?v=IcqCAqZtedI.javasc
ript:void(0);

Ward, Toby. "Beehive builds buzz at IBM." *Prescient Digital
Media*. Accessed June 5, 2013.
http://www.prescientdigital.com/articles/intranet-
articles/beehive-builds-buzz-at-ibm/.

Welch, Jack and Suzy Welch. "The Case for 20-70-10."
Bloomberg BusinessWeek. Published October 1, 2006.
Accessed June 6, 2013.
http://www.businessweek.com/stories/2006-10-
01/the-case-for-20-70-10.

Wikipedia. Accessed June 6, 2013. http://www.wikipedia.org/.

Wilson, Dominique. "Newark Mayor Cory Booker." *YouTube*.
Video, 0:30. Published December 28, 2010. Accessed
June 5, 2013.
http://www.youtube.com/watch?v=nqzhIX-mb5M.

About the Author

Ben Lichtenwalner is a follower of Christ, husband to an amazing wife, and father to two incredible boys. His studies of leadership span more than 10 years now and his work in business technology more than 15 years. Ben's experience also includes startups to Fortune 500 companies and some of the world's top non-profit organizations. Mr. Lichtenwalner considers himself fortunate to lead local and international employees, in-house and outsourced staff, as well as groups spanning many cultural and language borders.

Ben works to spread servant leadership awareness, adoption and action. He sees the power and opportunity of social media as a game changer for leaders. As a result, he's developed a unique perspective on the dovetail of leadership and social media. Find out more about Ben and his work at ModernServantLeader.com.

Made in the USA
Charleston, SC
27 December 2013